# Autism

## A Family Journey

## Cindy Rasmussen

KITSAP
PUBLISHING

**KITSAP PUBLISHING**

*Autism – A Family Journey*
First edition, published 2017

By Cindy Rasmussen
Cover images provided by Cindy Rasmussen
Copyright © 2017, Cindy Rasmussen

ISBN-978-1-942661-42-9

Published by Kitsap Publishing
P.O. Box 572
Poulsbo, WA 98370
www.KitsapPublishing.com

Printed in the United States of America

TD 20170313

50-10 9 8 7 6 5 4 3 2 1

# PREFACE

I wrote this story for my children to help them understand what happened in our family when they were growing up, from the perspective of a Mom. Our eldest son, Mark, was only 19 months old when our autistic son, Steven, was born and only 2 1/2 when the first serious problems began. Steven was 6 years old when Geoffrey was born. So although they were there for most of the journey, they have little memory or understanding of the most difficult years for our family. It is my hope that as adults they can read my account and gain a deeper insight and understanding into things that took place in their childhoods and that this knowledge might help them as they go forward in their own lives.

If you are the parent of an autistic child, I also want to share our story with you so that you know that you are not alone. Your journey will be different than ours because every child is an individual and every family is unique. Our story does not have a "happily ever after" ending, but it is a story of hope and encouragement. We have found no perfect solutions, and we made many mistakes along the way, but we have found ways to overcome the obstacles and to find joy and fulfillment in knowing and loving our autistic child. It is my hope that our story will encourage you to also find a rewarding journey in life.

For all who read this I would like to leave the message that autism is not just a scary label, it has a face and a personality. I want you to meet Steven, to get to know him as we do, and to learn why we love him and why he brings such joy to our lives and the lives of others. There are many "Stevens" out there, they are not all alike, but by knowing Steven through this story I hope to help readers have a greater understanding and acceptance of others like him.

*Cindy Rasmussen*

# CONTENTS

# PART I

## THE EARLY YEARS

# INTRODUCTION – FALL, 2009

It was a hot, windy day in Las Vegas. We were there because of Steven, our son, who was 39 at the time. He saves his money all year from his dishwashing job, so he can go on his annual "big trip". He always chooses the destination. Usually it is Disney World, but this year he chose Las Vegas. He likes the roller coaster at New York, New York; the gondola ride at Venice; the Tiger Zoo; Cirque de Soleil, and the swimming pool at the hotel.

I was sitting in the hotel hot tub and Phil, my husband, was swimming in the pool with Steven, but the wind kept blowing the pool chairs around, and the attendant was trying to collect them before they hit someone. Steven loves to swim and play on the pool slide and he was oblivious to this. There was a younger couple, probably in their early thirties, sharing the hot tub with me. They had been quietly talking to each other and observing Steven, who was coming over periodically to "check on Mom", making sure that I was still there.

Eventually the woman turned to me and asked if Steven is our son, to which I responded affirmatively. She then said, "Do you mind if I ask; is he autistic?". Her question did not surprise me, as we have become used to it. Her response when I told her that "Yes, he is autistic," was a little surprising though, as it is not what I usually hear. She told me that she had a young daughter who is also autistic. She and her husband were taking a much-needed vacation while a grandmother took care of their daughter for them, and she thought she recognized in Steven some of the telltale behaviors that characterize autism.

She was really interested in what adult autism looked like, and had many, many questions about what it had been like to raise a child with this disability. We talked for a very long time in spite of the increasing wind, and I tried to be reassuring, letting her know that there is life after autism, that it does improve with time, and that there can be many joys associated with watching this special needs child grow up. In many cases it is even more

3

rewarding than watching a normal child, because you are acutely aware of the severe struggles this child has to overcome in order to achieve some of the goals that come so easily to a normal child.

Finally the wind chased all of us inside, but I couldn't forget this conversation with a beautiful young woman, now in the midst of what would probably be the biggest challenge she and her husband would ever face. It brought back the memories of my own family's journey down this long and difficult road.

# IN THE BEGINNING

Phil and I had traveled to Denver to get married, and decided to spend a day on the ski slopes prior to our Big Day. Phil was an expert skier, while I was mediocre. I could do it, but NEVER attempted any slopes above beginner-intermediate level. We took the chair lift to what we thought was a slope I could manage, but at the top I looked down and all I could see were icy moguls and a VERY steep slope. I froze in place and told Phil I couldn't do it. He tried to coax me, telling me it would be easier than it looked from the top, and he knew I could do it. But I was really scared, and told him that I was going to walk down.

His response was, "If you walk down, I will not marry you!"

At that point I decided I would do it come hell or high water, and Phil very patiently stuck with me until we made it to the bottom safely, even though it took over an hour and he could have been down in about 15 minutes. Little did I know then that this was the first of many big challenging slopes that we would face in the life that we had decided to embark on together.

Two years earlier, I had graduated from the University of California, Berkeley with a degree in Sociology. I moved to San Diego, found a little apartment on the oceanfront, and started my first real job as a social worker for the Welfare Department of San Diego County.

Life was good, I loved my job and where I lived, and I was carefree and happy. The only empty spot was the lack of a special person to share my life. In less than a year, this empty spot was filled when I met Phil. He was a handsome young Naval Officer, a graduate of the Naval Academy at Annapolis, and currently an instructor in Basic Underwater Demolition Training, the elite Navy Special Forces now known as Navy SEALs.

After we were married, it seemed like life was complete. I dreamed of the little cottage with a white picket fence and the two of us happily watching two or three children growing up. It seemed like we would always be prosperous and successful together and that nothing could interrupt our happiness.

We purchased our first little house on the oceanfront on South Mission Beach in San Diego. We spent many hours tearing out walls, kitchen and bathroom, remodeling this little house in preparation for the arrival of our first little one. Mark, our first-born, arrived in July, 1969. He was beautiful and healthy; the dream of every first-time parent.

The first pinprick in my balloon occurred when Phil received orders for a year tour of duty in Vietnam. He had to leave at Thanksgiving when Mark was barely four months old. I was worried for Phil's safety and disappointed that he would miss almost the entire first year of our first child's life. But duty called, and I knew when I married a military officer that we would have separations.

Phil used to tell me that military wives were the happiest in the world – if they loved their husbands they were happy half of the time and unhappy the other half, and if they didn't love their husbands, the same half and half.

I packed up the house and went to Denver to stay with my parents for six of the 12 months he would be gone. Halfway through, we were allowed a week of R & R in Hawaii, so in the summer of 1970, Mark and I spent a wonderful week with Phil. I had not worried about birth control and within six weeks of returning home, I knew that I was pregnant again. While not planned, this pregnancy was also welcomed, as we felt it would be nice to have two children who could grow up close in age together.

*First, the two of us.*

*Then there were three.*

*Our first little house.*

# THE MEDICAL ODYSSEY

When I returned to San Diego, a friend invited me to have lunch with her, knowing I would be lonely and would enjoy spending time with friends while awaiting Phil's return. She had a little girl about the same age as Mark, so we thought the children would also enjoy playing together.

About a week after our lunch she called me with some rather disturbing news; her little girl had come down with the German measles (Rubella) and her pediatrician told her she should let me know, since I was in the first tri-mester of pregnancy. I was not really concerned, though, as I felt well and had no signs of illness. However, within the incubation period I became sick, and called my mother, who confirmed that I had not had Rubella as a child. My OB was on vacation, and his relief physician diagnosed me over the phone, telling me he thought it was simply an allergic reaction and rash.

Coincidentally, my sister Madelyn and her husband, Marvin, also a physician and a specialist in internal medicine, were coming to visit. When I picked them up at the airport I still had the rash; he took one look at it, and immediately pronounced that it was a measles rash. By this time my regular OB had returned from vacation, so when I went in for my next appointment he did a Titer Test for Rubella, which was positive.

When I was a social worker I had worked in the adoption agency for two years, and had learned about numerous birth defects, as many of the babies we dealt with were a result of high risk pregnancies. Therefore, I was well aware of what was known as "Rubella Syndrome" babies, and at this point I began to feel terrified about what lay ahead. Abortions were legal only under very narrowly defined circumstances and this was not one of them. Letters to Phil in Vietnam took over a month to go back and forth, so by the time he got the news, I was well into the second trimester of pregnancy, and beyond the point at which an abortion could be safely performed. My doctor told me that even if it had been legal, the risk to my health far outweighed the risk of having a baby with a birth defect, and that I should not even consider that option.

Phil returned home at Thanksgiving, a year after he left, and Steven joined our little family on March 2, 1971. We had outgrown our two-bedroom cottage by the beach and as much as we hated to do it, we decided to put the house up for sale. In less than 24 hours after listing it we had two solid offers and wondered if we should have asked a higher price. At any rate, we had already purchased a vacant lot on the bluff above the ocean in Solana Beach, and had planned to build on it "someday". "Someday" had arrived.

Phil was leaving the Navy in June, and we started planning a new life all over again. When June arrived, we had packed up the little house and turned it over to the new owners. Phil had not yet started a new career, and we had money in the bank that we had saved while he was away. My Mom offered to take care of the babies for us so that we could take a trip to Europe during this interlude in our lives.

It was my first time to go to Europe, and we had one of the most wonderful times of our lives on this trip. However, six weeks flew by and we had to return to reality. When we returned to Denver to collect the children from my Mom, she had some concerning news. Steven appeared to have a significant amount of abdominal pain, and was not having regular bowel movements. He sometimes went for a week without one, then exploded with foul-smelling diarrhea. He seemed perfectly normal otherwise, but this was a disturbing development.

We returned to San Diego and purchased an interim house to live in while we built our dream house. Steven's problem did not go away and in fact seemed to be getting more acute daily, so at our next regular visit to the pediatrician I asked him about it. When I was working at the adoption agency, there was a specific pediatrician on our panel who was skilled at diagnosing babies with problems and I had selected him to be our family's pedia-

10

trician. We were satisfied with his care for Mark, our firstborn, so there was no reason to believe that he wouldn't do a good job with Steven too.

After examining Steven, who at this time had an obviously very distended and abnormal tummy, the doctor turned to me and asked, "When did you start trying to potty train him?" I was stunned at first, then angry – how dare he accuse me of causing what appeared to be a serious problem for my baby. Mark, age two, was still in diapers, so I asked him why he thought I would even think of doing such a thing. He just shrugged his shoulders and said we should keep an eye on it.

Weeks went by with no improvement. The doctor examined him again and found nothing he was willing to treat, explaining to me that the test to determine if there was a problem was very expensive and very painful for Steven. The test he was referring to was a barium enema and he succeeded in dissuading me from proceeding with it. More weeks went by and I was becoming more frantic by the day. Finally, I phoned my sister, Madelyn, a nurse married to the doctor who had told me I had measles earlier. She invited me to come to San Francisco with the children and stay with them for a few days, giving me a break in my routine if nothing else. As soon as they saw Steven, both of them expressed great concern, and Marvin told me in no uncertain terms that I should insist on the diagnostic test and to do it immediately upon my return home.

In the meantime, Madelyn and I poured through the medical books reading about anything having to do with bowel disorders. Well, it didn't take us long to find a definitive diagnosis, even without having gone to medical school. The symptoms were classical and so evident we wondered how the pediatrician at home could have possibly missed it. She and I diagnosed Hirschsprung's Disease, a fairly rare bowel obstruction caused by a lack of nerve ending development in the large intestine. This prevents the normal bowel contractions which empty it out, called peristalsis. Surgical intervention is required to prevent death.

The tests were ordered, and I was in the waiting room at the hospital while the radiologist took the x-rays. After several long hours, the radiologist came over to talk to me. He started asking me questions about the symptoms I had observed over the months, and as I was talking his eyes grew wider and wider. Finally he asked me, "Have you EVER told anyone else about these symptoms?" I told him "Yes, I have been telling my pediatrician for months and he refused to listen to me". At this point he appeared to be angry and upset; he ended the interview, telling me to go home and phone the pediatrician as soon as I got there. He said there was a problem, and it was the pediatricians responsibility to explain it to me and to determine the next treatment steps.

Several days later the pediatrician reluctantly referred us to the best pediatric surgeon in town for an exam, but he also sabotaged the visit, setting me up as the frantic, neurotic mother who had self-diagnosed her child and was insisting on unnecessary treatment. Unfortunately, I was still naïve enough to believe that the medical profession was almost godlike in its ability to diagnose and cure illness. I was in for a rude awakening. The surgeon knew that something was definitely wrong, but wanted more tests. He first sent us for a biopsy locally, then referred us to the medical center at UCLA for another barium enema and biopsy. When ALL of these tests came back as positive for Hirschsprung's Disease, the surgery was finally scheduled.

The procedure was explained to us; a very difficult and fairly high risk surgery. It would take four to five hours in the OR; Dr. C., the surgeon, was the only doctor in a six-state radius who was qualified to perform it (children needing this procedure were flown in from all over the western U.S. for him to do it). It was a two part procedure, and the second part would be done six weeks later. Steven would require intensive recovery care, so my Mom came to stay with us to take care of Mark while I took care of Steven, both while he was in the hospital and at home.

The dreaded day arrived. Steven was taken away to the OR, and I was left sitting in the waiting room of Children's Hospital.

Phil was beside me, but neither of us said anything. We were both frozen in fear; our beautiful baby could lose his life on this day. Our world was shattering around us and we had no control over it. All we could do was sit and wait.

Hours later, and after what seemed like an eternity, Doctor C. appeared in the doorway. He was smiling and relief flooded through us. Steven had survived the surgery and appeared to be doing well. We were not out of the woods; there would be a long recovery, but things were looking good.

Steven was finally home from the hospital. He had a small stump protruding from his rectum where healthy tissue containing normal nerve endings had been pulled through the lower intestine from above and needed to heal in place before the second surgery could be performed. The second surgery was to trim the stump away, giving Steven a normal rectum and hopefully a normally functioning intestinal system.

Six weeks later we were back in the hospital, but this time we were feeling optimistic about the outcome. Yes, everything went well, and after a short recovery time we were home again. For a while, everything appeared to be fine, but several weeks later Steven started exhibiting signs of abdominal distress again. He was having diarrhea again and screamed in pain after every meal. First we visited the pediatrician, who was taking no chances this time, and immediately referred us back to the surgeon. Dr. C., the surgeon could not find anything wrong, so he sent us home with instructions to keep an eye on things, and advise him if any changes. More days went by, finally turning into several weeks. The constant screaming was driving me insane, so Phil told me to hire a babysitter so he could take me out to dinner one night. The report from the sitter when we returned: "He screamed the entire time you were gone, there is something terribly wrong".

It was now a long holiday weekend. It was excruciating to watch Steven screaming in pain 24/7. Then one day something changed for the worst. He started to vomit EVERYTHING! He couldn't keep down even a sip of water. He was slipping away in front of our eyes. I called the pediatrician in a panic; he was reluctant to come into his office on this holiday, but sensed the urgency in my voice. When I met him there, he took one look at Steven and sent us immediately to the hospital. Dr. C. was called; he met us at the hospital and practically grabbed Steven out of my arms rushing him to the OR.

Once more Phil and I were sitting stonily in the waiting room, not knowing if we would see our child alive again. I was too numb even to cry, but my heart was breaking inside. A nurse came out and explained to us that they were doing exploratory surgery, and that it would probably take about an hour. Two hours went by, then three and finally four before Dr. C. appeared. He was not smiling, but looked relieved as he sat down beside us to talk. He explained that Steven had developed an Intussusception, a condition where the small intestine telescopes back inside itself and causes a total obstruction of the upper bowel. This condition normally requires immediate surgical intervention or the patient will die; but Steven's had been there for so long that it had grown together before he presented the first diagnostic symptom, the vomiting. Dr. C. had never seen this before, and was amazed that Steven had survived it.

Life seemingly returned to a degree of normalcy. After getting out of the Navy, Phil joined a small group of friends who wanted to form a construction company and build "spec houses". The real estate market was booming, and Phil had done enough construction that he was a self-taught contractor. One of his first projects was the construction of our own oceanfront house in Solana Beach. We built it with our own cash, and were living in it still uncompleted, but we were young and adventurous, so we did not complain.

Steven had seemingly recovered from the surgeries, although there were still some residual symptoms that were worrisome. Then one day, he started vomiting again, but in an effort not to panic, I waited to make sure that he didn't just have the flu. As the hours went by, it was apparent that he was in trouble again, so once more we rushed him to the hospital. He was severely dehydrated with acidosis when we got there, and had to be given IV fluids before any further treatment could be commenced. After he was stabilized, Dr. C. determined that the problem was due to the way in which his sphincter muscle was contracting, and that it was causing another obstruction. Steven needed yet another surgery, as the involuntary sphincter needed an excision in order to release it and relieve the obstruction. The result was a lifelong problem of bowel control, but after that Steven did not require any further surgery, and gradually recovered from all of the multiple hospitalizations.

As an adult, he has done remarkably well in managing his bowel control. He has occasional leakage, but no noticeable outward symptoms.

*Welcoming baby Steven.*

*Visiting Grandma in Denver.*

*Mark "helping" feed Steven.*

*Steven at nine months.*

*Early development - Pre-surgery: 8-11 months*

# DIAGNOSIS: AUTISM

After a few years, the construction company Phil was involved with disbanded. There were the "to be expected" disagreements with several members deciding they wanted to do other things, so everyone parted as friends and went about their own lives. Phil decided to form his own business as a general contractor, and I became the "stay-at-home Mom", trying to help him run the business from our house. He was out everyday, all day, doing the physical labor of building homes, while I ran the office part of the business at home. Once more our lives took on a semblance of normalcy and routine, although it was difficult to find "together" time. He worked long hours and came home tired every night. I also had my hands full chasing two toddlers, answering phones, and doing the paperwork required for running a business with six to nine employees at any given time.

It is impossible to know when the signs of trouble with Steven began to appear. It would have been like watching a new flower bud open or a seed sprout; the changes were so slow as to be imperceptible at first, but suddenly the flower opens, or the seed sprouts and starts growing, and you are fully aware of what is happening.

There were little things at first that were easy to ignore. Steven had started saying a few words before he had all of his surgeries, which happened when he was between the ages of 14 months and 24 months; then he stopped trying to talk. At his regular visits to the pediatrician, we talked about his slow development, but the pediatrician attributed it to the trauma of the illnesses and all of the hospitalizations. In several of those hospitalizations, Steven's hands had had to be restrained to the side of the bed so that he could not pull out the IV's, certainly a traumatizing event for a two-year-old toddler who has no idea what is happening to him.

I wanted to believe the pediatrician, that Steven's slow development of language and social skills was a result of all of his previous medical traumas but the months passed and the two year old turned three. He was still not talking. I continued to deny to myself and others that there was a problem, stating that he just needed time to outgrow this stage he was going through.

However, we started to notice that he often seemed unable to give us his attention when we were trying to engage him. He also started to exhibit extreme tantrum behavior. I knew what normal two-year-old tantrums looked like; Mark was now close to four years old, so I had been there, done that. But Steven's tantrums had a whole new dimension. His crying was an ear-piercing scream, sounding almost like an animal instead of a little boy. And he could do it for hours at a time without a break. He also exhibited an inability to entertain himself with normal play activities, or to be able to play with other children in a normal way, including his big brother.

As the tantrums began to take over our lives, I was forced to recognize that we had a problem, but what it was I didn't have a clue. I knew he wasn't retarded because he could put together puzzles far above his age level and in a record amount of time. I also knew that even though he wasn't talking, he understood everything I said because of his responses when I talked to him. As a student of sociology and psychology, I had studied a little about autism in school, but didn't think that Steven's behavior fit the picture I had in my mind from those brief studies. I was picturing a child sitting in a corner, facing the wall, totally disengaged with anything going on around him and making repetitive hand-wringing movements, or banging his head against the wall over and over completely unaware of any pain. Steven had none of those behaviors.

Months passed and the behaviors he did exhibit became increasingly difficult. Physically, Steven was extraordinarily strong and athletically adept. He was able to climb a four-foot-high fence in our backyard and walk along the top of it like a tightrope. We had an upstairs loft area that was open to our lower floor and supported by 10-foot-tall I-beams. Steven was able to shimmy up and down those beams in order to get to the second story without using the stairs.

He started to develop repetitive activities, one of which was playing with water. He would pour a bucket of water from one container to another over and over again, laughing in glee as he watched it pour. He was also fearless, with no concept of danger at all. His obsession with water led to some pretty intense moments of fear for us, however, as he would run away from our house looking for swimming pools in the neighborhood, which were abundant. And since he could seemingly scale almost any fence, he had no trouble entering a neighboring yard with a pool even though it was fenced.

He developed some annoying behaviors too. He would run around the house turning the light switches on and off for hours. He constantly opened the refrigerator door looking for sweets, and spilling the contents of the refrigerator onto the floor, with lots of broken jars and liquid spills for me to clean up. I needed to go shopping at the grocery store and take the children with me, and this started turning into a nightmare trip for me. Steven rode in the basket and grabbed at items as we went by, especially candy or cookies, then had a tantrum if I said "no". His screaming was so intense that I often needed to leave the store before I was finished shopping. I learned to take some candy with me in my purse, and whenever he opened his mouth to scream, I popped a candy in it to appease him, just so that I could get through the shopping trip.

We were no longer able to take family outings, as the tantrums were too disruptive, especially in public settings. He was extremely quick, and would be gone in a flash if you looked the other direction for even a second. Over time it seemed as if we were captives in our own home, and we were more and more becoming slaves to Steven's dysfunctional behaviors.

Since he had no fear and no concept of danger, my days became nightmarish just watching over him every minute of every day. He also seemed never to sleep and eventually took over our nights. He wandered around the house at night, and we worried that he would go outside and become lost in the dark. Our house was in a particularly dangerous location, as it was perched on a 90 foot high bluff above the ocean. Even though the play yard was on the street side with no access to the bluff, and we installed childproof locks on all of the doors and windows on the inside, Steven still managed to escape.

One day the next door neighbor rang the doorbell in the middle of the day and told me that one of the children was on a ledge approximately 10 feet below the top of the bluff. Of course it was Steven. One misstep, and he would fall to his death below on the beach. There was no time to do anything except try to reach him before he could, so the neighbor and I approached him carefully. The neighbor climbed down to him and handed him up to me. I had thought he was in his room napping, but he had unlocked the window and climbed out.

I was frantic about how to protect him, so Phil suggested we put bars on his bedroom window. We also removed the interior door to his room and installed a heavy screen door that we could lock from the outside, so that he was unable to come out of his room at night or nap time, but we could still see and hear him.

On another occasion, after we installed the bars, a low-flying helicopter was buzzing the beach in the middle of the night shining a searchlight up and down the bluff. Our bedroom window faced the beach, so the light woke us up, and made us wonder what was happening outside. Less than half an hour later our doorbell rang, and we were greeted by two Sheriff's Deputies. They asked if we had a disabled child in the home, and if we knew where he was. My heart stopped. Could Steven have possibly gotten through that barred window and fallen off the bluff? I raced to his room to check on him, and thankfully he was there and sleeping soundly. With relief we informed the officers that he was okay and asked what had prompted their search. Apparently a neighbor whom we didn't know personally, was aware of

Steven's presence in the neighborhood. She had heard loud crying noises on the bluff and called the Deputies thinking it might be Steven. It turns out that it was a cat or cats, but still we were grateful for her concern and their response.

The stress was taking a toll on our marriage. Phil was working ever longer hours, and I suspected he simply didn't want to be at home because it was too stressful. I was exhausted at the end of the day, so our communication turned into a review of problems at night, not much fun for either of us. The more he was gone, the more I felt angry at the lack of support, and so things continued to deteriorate. It finally reached a point where I told him I was finished, that I would take the kids and go home to Denver until I could re-group my life. He voluntarily sought out a marriage counselor, and so I stayed and we agreed to work on our problems.

We were both left wondering whatever had happened to our lives. We had started out with so much hope and so many dreams for our future, and here we were with shattered lives discussing a divorce. The saving grace is that we both loved our children and had deep concerns about their future if we did not stay together. Even if we didn't love each other at that place in time, we both still cared about the other. It was mainly that we were both exhausted and we didn't know what on earth we could do to "fix it". The one thing we did know is that we had to find out what was wrong with Steven and get him some help. So we agreed to stay together and continue to work on our family problems. As of this writing, we are still together after 49 years of marriage. Miraculously, we have survived the storms and chaos of living with autism.


*FALL, 1974*

In the summer of this year, my wonderful sister and her doctor husband had been to our home for a visit, and had observed first-hand Steven's behavior. They had not rendered an opinion as to what they thought was wrong, but at about the time I was at the end of my rope, Madelyn sent me an article from a recent medical journal describing the latest research on autism. The article went into explicit detail about the symptoms, various tests that had been conducted, and the latest research on innovative treatment methods. The further I read, the more I cried, as it was very clear that Steven was in fact autistic. Madelyn and Marvin had known after they had stayed with us, but hadn't wanted to be the ones to tell us, at least not then. They wanted us to seek an expert opinion and also to find some help for Steven and ourselves. I had been trying to convince myself that it couldn't possibly be true, how could that happen to us? Hadn't we already "paid our dues" with his severe physical problems? But now I really had to face the truth, and in some ways it was a relief to finally know what we were dealing with.

The article in the journal described the work of a world renowned expert in autism, Dr. Ivar Lovaas, who was conducting studies at the UCLA Neuropsychiatric Institute. He had obtained grants for his study and they were accepting patients. Within days I had scheduled an appointment for Steven to be seen at the clinic. In order for him to be accepted in the study, I needed to take him to Los Angeles for about six visits scheduled one or two weeks apart. This was a small price to pay for being able to obtain this expert help, so we agreed without hesitation.

However, getting back and forth to Los Angeles with Steven was no easy task. Just as he was an escape artist at home, he was also a Houdini about getting out of his car seat; he had no compunctions about opening a car door while we were in motion. Phil had to work and was unable to accompany me on most of these trips, as it took all day. That meant I had to be able to contain Steven in the car seat for the two hour trip down, and the same for back home again while driving in LA freeway traffic. I had to stay in the far right lane as much as possible in case I had to suddenly pull off the freeway, which did happen on one of the trips. There were no child locks on the car doors as these had yet to be invented, so I tried to tie him securely into the car seat, but he still managed to open the door on one occasion.

The tests were finally finished; I had given volumes of medical records to the clinic and answered pages of questions about early development and behaviors. Steven had undergone hearing tests, vision tests, blood tests, IQ testing and multiple psychological tests. Although we did not speak to him directly, Dr. Lovaas had completed an observation session of Steven's behavior. The verdict was in, but I already knew what it was and I was anxious to talk about the treatment.

Yes, Steven was classically autistic. There was no ambiguity about the diagnosis and no sugarcoating the prognosis. Steven was now 3 ½ years old, and if he didn't begin talking before the age of four, the prognosis was dim; he would likely need to be institutionalized eventually, as he probably would not be able to function in normal society.

UCLA Neuropsychiatric Institute had an inpatient unit and wanted to keep him there for six months so they could begin a treatment plan. I couldn't imagine leaving my child in the hospital again, so options were discussed. Phil and I knew about an outpatient treatment facility in San Diego and wanted to try that first. Yes, the staff at UCLA knew about the Los Niños Center, and believed it was a good quality treatment center and would be an appropriate alternative for him. They encouraged us to enroll him in that Center.

*Our new house - Solana Beach.*

*Steven scaling backyard fence.*

*Steven playing.*

*Steven's backyard and water fascination.*

# LOS NIÑOS

## OCTOBER, 1974

I contacted the Los Niños Center and Steven was accepted into the program. At our first interview with the staff, they asked me for a description of Steven's behavior. Their response was the most welcome news I had heard in months: "We are not concerned about how bad his behavior is, we accept the children whom no one else is willing to take, and we can help you." I think my relief at this news was audible. We filled out the required paper work, and we were informed that for the first three weeks we would be driving Steven to Los Niños and picking him up four hours later, with no opportunity for observation or visiting. They needed this introductory time for intensive therapy with Steven and no parental interference. Needless to say, I readily agreed. The school was 25 miles from our home, so I would be driving 100 miles daily to take him to school; a small price to pay for some precious hours of relief and some effective help.

DAY ONE: I took Steven to school, dropped him off and heard him starting to scream as I was walking away. I was sad that we had to do this, but I kept walking. Four hours later I returned to pick him up. He was sitting by himself in a small room with a teacher, facing the wall and on the blackboard was written, "Steven screaming: 3 hours, 50 minutes".

DAY TWO: I took Steven to school, dropped him off and once more heard him start to scream. Four hours later I picked him up, same scene as the day before, but written on the blackboard was: Steven screaming: 3 hours, 15 minutes.

DAY THREE: I took Steven to school, dropped him off and heard him start to cry, not scream. Four hours later I picked him up and on the blackboard: Steven screaming: 2 hours.

DAY FOUR: I took Steven to school and it was quiet as I left. Four hours later I picked him up, the teacher was smiling and on the blackboard was written: Steven screaming: 5 minutes.

This was the initial breakthrough that must occur before any progress could be made in the treatment program. Now we were ready to move on to the next step.

After Steven was enrolled and during the three week initial introduction period, several members of the staff conducted an observation session of Steven at home. During the session they asked me to name ONE specific behavior that we would like to change. After all of us considered various choices (I wanted to change everything!), we settled on his poor eating habits. His limited diet consisted of bologna sandwiches and anything sweet, period!! The strategy we developed would be another trying emotional experience for Steven and me. Initially he was not allowed to eat breakfast before school because he was rewarded for behavioral progress at school with food. We decided that he would be offered a cheese sandwich at lunch, NOT BOLOGNA! If he refused to eat the sandwich, he would go home hungry after school. He would then be offered the sandwich for dinner, and if not eaten, would go to bed hungry. He would be offered the cheese sandwich again at school, and same result if not eaten. We checked with the pediatrician before embarking on this program, particularly in light of Steven's earlier digestive system problems. But the physician assured us that he would be fine as long as he drank plenty of liquids. And so we started down this difficult road.

DAY ONE: Steven refused the sandwich at school and went home hungry. He refused it at dinner and went to bed hungry.

DAY TWO: Steven refused the sandwich at school and went home hungry. He refused again at dinner.

DAY THREE: Same as day two.

DAY FOUR: Same. I was getting really worried and called the pediatrician for more reassurance that this would be okay. I was told to continue.

DAY FIVE: The School Administrator greeted me as I got out of the car, and said, "Come here, you have to see this". As we approached the room where Steven waited for me, he was literally GOBBLING the cheese sandwich!!!

This was the huge treatment breakthrough that everyone had been waiting for. Every behavior change that we attempted from this point on became progressively easier to accomplish.

There were two more behaviors that we wanted to target next. The first was opening and closing the refrigerator at home all day long, taking food in and out, and often spilling it and breaking jars on the floor. It seemed like I was spending hours every day just cleaning up messes in the kitchen, so the new rule was that Steven was not allowed in the refrigerator. Every time he approached it, I had to stand in front of the door and issue a loud verbal "No". At first, as soon as I moved away from the door he would be back. When I frustrated his attempt he would tantrum, but eventually he gave it up for a slightly longer period of time. The intervention required that I literally guard the refrigerator door until he stopped making attempts to open it. If he was to be successful, then it would be 10 times more difficult to get him to stop. So I persevered, which meant standing in the kitchen all day for the first day. On the second day he made a few weak attempts, then amazingly he gave it up!!!

The second behavior that was driving all of us crazy was the constant flicking of light switches. Steven loved watching the flickering of the lights at night, so would run around the house turning them on and off whether or not we were in the room and using the light. So once more I became a "guardian", this time of the light switches. Thankfully, this "lesson" lasted about half the time as the refrigerator operation.

31

# THE PROGRAM

Los Niños means "the children" in Spanish and the Los Niños Education Center was founded in 1971 by Vista Hill Foundation, a non-profit organization that provided mental health services and services to those with developmental disabilities. Dr. Anne Donnellan was the first Director of the Center and was a nationally known expert on autism. The program was modeled after the behavior modification methods pioneered by Dr. Ivar Lovaas at the UCLA Neuropsychiatric Institute. At that time, there was little understanding about autism, and even less about its treatment. Less than a decade earlier it was considered by many to be caused by "cold mothers" who failed to love their children, thereby causing the children to suffer from extreme withdrawal. This notion of causation was difficult to dispel, and vestiges still remained as late as the early 1970's in some circles. Parents of autistic children found it extremely difficult to get an accurate diagnosis, much less to find any meaningful help with treatment. The pioneering work done by Dr. Lovaas with behavior modification was a breakthrough in treatment, and while there was no cure, his work did prove to make a significant difference in the ability of autistic children to function. Therefore, we considered our family to be extremely fortunate to find the Los Niños Center in our hometown of San Diego offering his treatment methods as an outpatient facility. Los Niños was in its third year of existence at the time that Steven was enrolled. Dr. Donnellan left for a new opportunity shortly after Steven arrived, and Dr. Elizabeth M. took over the program.

Liz was one of the most beautiful people I have ever known. As director of the program, it was so much more than a career position for her; it was a labor of love. She instinctively understood what life was like for our families with autistic children even though she had no children of her own. Her demeanor was very calm and soothing, and she was always available to listen to our problems and offer any help that she could to us. Liz once mentioned to me that at this time she had no children. Later, when some of us were visiting informally after we dropped off our children at school, one of the mothers asked Liz if she had any children. Without thinking twice I responded immediately, "Yes, she has 20 of them right here at the school, and we are all so grateful that we have her here". Everyone smiled and nodded their heads in agreement. It would have been difficult for any of us to imagine that school without Liz.

Other staff members included three or four Special Ed teachers, at least three paid teacher assistants, an occupational therapist and numerous volunteers, some from local universities who were interested in studying autism and/or Special Ed services. There was an "on call" speech therapist who came at least once a week, so that all of the children received speech therapy, and the teachers received consulting services. The school provided a multi-faceted approach to treatment, with a heavy emphasis on behavior modification. The underlying philosophy of behavior modification is that most behavior is learned, and that positive and negative reinforcements can facilitate the learning of functional behaviors and the extinguishment of negative behaviors.

Most autistic children seem unable to sort out sensory input in the brain in a way that makes sense, and therefore it is believed that the world they experience is overwhelming, and frightening. They respond by becoming totally dependent on a rigid environment which to them is manageable. They need to have "sameness" in every aspect of their lives. This includes the exact same daily routine, the same placement of objects in their environment, taking the same routes everyplace they go, eating the same foods all of the time, and having the same people around them all of the time. If there are any departures from this structured environment the result is usually an out-of-control temper tantrum. They are simply unable to tolerate any change at all. Therefore, they become unable to learn any new information even though they are usually capable of doing so. The challenge then becomes finding ways to break through this rigidity so that learning can take place. They need to be able to develop the skills they need to expand their experiences so that they can continue to learn and grow and cope with life in the greater outside world.

At the same time, autistic children seem to have no ability to discern danger or to learn how to approach new situations with caution. They will do things like run in the street with no awareness of approaching vehicles, go outside in the snow without a jacket, or climb a tree with no awareness that a branch might not hold their weight and they could fall. They also seem not to feel pain or discomfort. For example, when Steven was about 3 ½, he fell on our front porch, hitting the edge of a wood stair with his chin and splitting the chin wide open. It was late in the afternoon of Christmas Eve day, probably one of the most inconvenient days of the year for a medical emergency, but it was immediately obvious that we needed to get medical attention for the wound. The pediatrician's office was about 10 minutes from our home, and Dr. W., one of the partner physicians in the practice, was there. We went to the office, he took a look at the chin and groaned. He admitted that one of his least favorite things as a doctor was putting stitches in children's cuts. Steven was an especially difficult case, as he was terrified of doctors, hospitals and medical settings in general.

After we were able to subdue him and calm him down, Dr. W. administered a local anesthesia, stitched up the wound, and sent us on our way. I strapped Steven into the car seat in the back, and drove the ten minutes to our home. When I parked and lifted him out of his seat I was astounded and dismayed to discover that he had quietly pulled out every stitch during the short drive home!!!! Needless to say, we turned right around and went back to the doctors office to re-do those stitches, but this time we found a pair of cotton mittens to put securely on BOTH HANDS so that the stitches would stay in; and the mittens were worn day and night until the wound healed and the stitches dissolved.

Therefore, the first task at the Los Niños Center was to break the pattern of rigidity that Steven had set up for himself. Those who treated autistic children had learned that if you could break through the pattern with one specific behavior, then it became easier to generalize the breakthrough to other behaviors. They also learned that the best way to break the dysfunctional behavior was to "non-attend" to it. That is why, when Steven screamed when being left at the center without me, they had put him in a chair facing the wall, in a room with no one except one monitor, who ignored him. He was allowed to scream as long as he wanted to, with no consequences. Since he received no attention, i.e. "no positive reinforcement", for the screaming, he eventually gave it up. He was then ready for the next step in the treatment plan, which was to break at least one of his rigid routines, the eating of the same food all of the time, his bologna sandwich.

It became apparent through this process how strongly the autistic person needs rigidity for his very survival. Steven was willing to give up food, one of the most necessary primal survival needs, for four days before he would break the pattern. However, once it was broken, he was able to quickly generalize the behavior to other rituals that needed to change. Stopping the ritual of opening and closing the refrigerator door, and flicking the light switches on and off became progressively easier.

After some of the basic dysfunctional behaviors are under control the next thing autistic children need to learn is how to focus on a task in order to master it. Once more the inability to sort out sensory input interferes with learning. The areas of the brain that develop language skills are the most severely affected in most autistic children, and this leads to other outstanding deficiencies, such as the ability to interact socially with other people. To further complicate the issue, other disabilities can and do co-exist with autism, such as mental retardation. Therefore, there is a wide spectrum of autism disorders, and the levels of functioning of autistic people  fall along a continuum from very severe to almost normal.

The Los Niños Center was the first and the only one of its kind in Southern California at the time when Steven started there in

1974. It had approximately 20 children enrolled, ranging in age from 2½ years to 12 years old, and ranging in levels of functioning from very low to approaching normal. At that time there were no facilities in the public schools for teaching autistic children, so the only available options would be a school like Los Niños, or an institution for the mentally ill and disabled, or trying to raise your child alone at home with no professional help. The children at Los Niños were divided into small groups depending on their level of functioning, and the ratio of staff to children was 1 to 1 most of the time.

Steven was in the lowest-level class when he arrived. Although he understood much of what we said to him (which is termed receptive language), at age 3 ½ he had no expressive language. When he was diagnosed at UCLA, I was informed that if he did not develop language by the age of four, chances were very slight that he ever would, and his quality of life would be greatly diminished. This information was again reinforced when we enrolled him at Los Niños, although they were experimenting at the time with teaching sign language. I was having difficulty accepting this prognosis, and established my own personal deadline to see that Steven acquired language by the time he was four.

Steven's first lesson was learning to "look at me" when prompted by a teacher. In the beginning, there were two people working with him in short sessions. He sat in a little chair, with one person behind him and one in front. The person in front would give the prompt to "look at me", taking his face in her hands and forcing him to do so. Then the person in back would pop a tiny bite of an M & M in his mouth, praising him with "good looking". This session lasted about 5 minutes and was repeated intermittently throughout the day until there was a measurable positive result. He needed to attend to the prompt successfully a given number of times and for a certain time period.

In my observation of the work being done at the center, I learned that imitation is a very important aspect of learning, especially for these non-verbal children, and unless they learned to imitate

37

they would never learn how to speak. So a large part of Steven's day was spent teaching him to observe and imitate, something that normal children do naturally, but that autistic children have to painstakingly learn.

Another strategy used for teaching language skills was to place three familiar objects on the table in front of Steven. He was asked to "point to the ball", then he was physically prompted by moving his hand to the ball, and rewarded with the M & M combined with verbal praise. This was also repeated until there was measurable success; Steven pointed to the ball correctly when asked to do so and without the physical prompt. After the three week "no visiting" period was up, I made it a point to observe as many of Steven's sessions as I could, so that I could work with him at home after school hours and on weekends. The staff encouraged parents to participate as much as they wanted to, so after a short time of observation, I was receiving "homework assignments" for Steven and spent many hours teaching as many pre-language skills as I could.

Prior to our arrival at the school, parents had not been encouraged to volunteer at the school, but after I had been there visiting and observing Steven, I decided to ask if I could also do some volunteering. The staff decided there was no reason not to let me do that, but they wanted me to work in a different classroom than Steven's, so I now had the opportunity to work with and observe the teaching methods employed for the higher-level functioning children. I was delighted to be involved at that level so that I could learn how to work with Steven at home on some of the more skilled tasks that I felt he was capable of doing.

While we were working at school on shaping and imitating sounds, and doing rudimentary drawings of simple everyday objects, such as a house or a stick person, I started working with Steven at home on learning and drawing the letters of the alphabet. Steven loved it and was a very fast learner. He was learning to imitate simple words at school, which was very exciting for all of us, and I was also teaching him to write and spell some of

38

these same words. I did not tell the staff what I was doing with him at home until I felt there was real progress, so when I finally showed them how well he was able to write and spell words, they were astounded. Not long after that he was "graduated" to the medium-level class. This was a thrilling day for all of us; we now knew that Steven was going to learn to speak and understand language, and would not be confined to life in an institution.

After that he learned simple math, addition and subtraction, and eventually he learned to read. Everything he learned was at first by rote, but as he progressed, his skills became more practical and useful, and he had an understanding of the concepts behind the rote memorization. As I watched Steven slowly learning things that came so easily and so naturally for other children, I gained a sense of what a miracle it really is that normal children can learn these skills with such ease.

In addition to learning new skills, autistic children have to also unlearn the dysfunctional behaviors that they have acquired for coping in an overwhelming world that they don't understand. Before Steven had been diagnosed, when he was grabbing at all of the sweets in the grocery store and I placated him by feeding him candy to keep him from throwing a loud temper tantrum, I was reinforcing the bad behavior; so of course he learned to scream often and loudly whenever he didn't get his way about things.

He also had acquired a habit of biting every time someone said "no"; his way of expressing his frustration at not getting his way. Well, it got so bad that he would bite a perfect stranger in public if he heard the word "no" in a casual conversation. This was obviously unacceptable and had to be dealt with sooner rather than later. The Los Niños staff and Phil and I had a "brainstorming session" to find a strategy to "extinguish" this very bad habit. Although some of the children responded to "negative" reinforcement to extinguish bad behaviors, Steven did not accept this very well. We felt that he had experienced too much pain during his many hospital stays, and that any negative punishments that were administered had the effect of setting him back in the program rather than helping him move forward. So we determined that the best way to deal with the dysfunctional behaviors was to "non-attend", such as being put in a "time-out". However, we struggled for a long time with the biting and found that "time out" did not work, so we needed to develop a different strategy. Finally, a staff member came up with the idea that if Steven was wearing a catcher's mask used in baseball, that he would be physically unable to bite himself or anyone else, and it would not be necessary for another person to apply a physical restraint. This was a brilliant idea and worked like a charm. Sessions with Steven were then commenced whereby he was prompted to do a task that everyone knew he could not do, and when he gave an incorrect response a loud "no" was issued. Predictably, he became frustrated and upset, tried to bite, and was unable to do so with the mask on. Once more, this task was repeated intermittently during the day for a number of days until finally he quit responding by trying to bite. He was tested over a longer period of time in a controlled situation without the mask, and finally the behavior was permanently gone. Whew!!!

*Sample drawings - May 8, 1978. Teacher: He chose what to draw*

41

*Steven working and playing with teacher - Los Ninos*

*Steven working with teacher*

*Mom working with Steven at home*

# THE MOTHERS' GROUP

When Steven enrolled in Los Niños, I began to spend inordinate amounts of time driving. The school was 25 miles each way, so I made two round trips of 50 miles, or a total of 100 miles a day. Most of the parents lived a little closer to the Center than we did, but some of them had a journey nearly as long as mine. Liz kindly offered those of us who drove long distances the opportunity to have a cup of coffee after we dropped off our children, so Karen B. and I started spending time talking to each other several mornings a week, depending on our individual schedules. Karen was a very attractive young mother about my same age and educational level, so we found that we had much in common. She was from Germany and had married her American husband when he was stationed there in the Army. She had two little girls, about the same ages as my two boys, and it was her older daughter who was autistic.

I had not realized until Karen and I became friends how alone and isolated parents become when they have a child with autism. The child's behavior is so disturbing that families stop going anywhere in public unless it is something they absolutely have to do, like shop for groceries. They no longer visit friends because it simply is impossible to do so; the child is too out of control, and the friends' homes might be "child-proofed" but they are not "autism-proofed". Likewise, the parents stop inviting friends to their homes because it is too chaotic to do so. Husbands and wives stop going out together because there is no one who can babysit for them, and families no longer take vacations because of the inability to do anything in public. Even trying to visit on the phone becomes next to impossible, because the autistic child demands constant attention and monitoring.

It is perhaps this feeling of isolation that is the most damaging and destructive to families of autistic children. So when Steven first started going to the Los Niños Center, I was still in a very dark place, but as I started meeting others with the same problem,

I experienced a great sense of relief. I was no longer alone with the problem. There were other mothers out there who understood and experienced the same things that I was going through. And there were other families that were struggling like we were to just make it through each day.

As time went on, Karen and I invited other mothers to join us for coffee in the morning, and before long we had a little group of about four "regulars". At this point Liz would sometimes join us and took great interest in our discussions of life with autism. So she asked us if we would like to have a regular once-a-week mothers' meeting if the Center provided a place for us. We were delighted to have that opportunity, and an invitation was issued for any parents or other interested caregivers to join us for our weekly meeting. There was an overwhelming response; every caregiver of a child at the Center participated in as many of our meetings as they were able to attend!!

We talked not only about the problems of dealing with the behaviors of our autistic children, but also our concerns about our normal children, and how worried we were about what was happening to them. We also talked about our marriages, and the effect this disorder can have on them. A number of mothers had already lost their marriages and were trying to cope alone, so it was helpful to them to know that they were supported by all of us, and that they shouldn't consider themselves to be failures because their marriages had been unable to survive this very severe disorder.

Most importantly, we learned to laugh again. We learned that even the most dysfunctional antics of our children were sometimes very funny. Together we learned to have a sense of humor about many of the things that went on in our homes. I remember once around Christmas time, when our little group was fairly new, I came in and opened the discussion by asking, "How many of you have the 'Falling Christmas Tree Syndrome' at your house?" There was a moment of stunned silence, then everyone burst out laughing. It turned out that everyone had been struggling with the same problem. Our autistic children were all fascinated by the lights and glitter on the trees, and were pulling the trees over in their excitement to touch the ornaments and lights. Things that once seemed so disastrous were now funny.

It is thought by some experts that autistic children do not know how to tell a lie because their understanding of the world is based on very concrete experiences. They learn from what they can actually see, hear, and touch, but abstract ideas for the most part are incomprehensible to them. Therefore, they do not have the ability to plan ahead in a way that would be deceptive. However, we caught Steven in several deceptions that were very funny, since his attempts were so rudimentary. On one occasion when Steven was about 5 years old he was wearing a swimming suit and heading out of the front door with his skateboard under his arm. He saw me coming and immediately said, "No go swimming". He had an excellent memory and knew the locations of every swimming pool within a two to three mile radius of our home. He also knew how to ride his skateboard to get to them quickly. So it was really funny to have him tell me that he was not going swimming!!

He also used to carry water in a little bucket from the kitchen to the backyard where he created a mud hole and tracked it back into the house. The trip required that he go through the family room between the sofa and the TV. We had placed that particular activity "off limits" primarily due to the mess it created, but also we wanted him to expand his repertoire of play activities. One evening the rest of the family was sitting on the sofa watching TV when Steven traipsed through the family room between us and the TV with his little bucket of water, stooping low as he went. It was so funny watching him trying to "keep a low profile" so that we wouldn't notice him as he ran right in front of us.

Our mothers' group realized that we could create some social activities for our families that we had previously been deprived of, such as a Halloween party and a Christmas party. We involved our men in the planning and production of these parties, and all of our children had a blast. It was the first time in many months, and in some cases years, that our families had been able to enjoy having fun together. If an autistic child decided to tantrum, no one even looked twice. And actually the tantrums were few because the children were in a familiar setting at the Center with staff and family that they knew well.

As time went on, Liz became acquainted with a medical student who was specializing in psychiatry, and was very interested in our Mother's Group. Liz asked if we would mind having her join the group, and soon she was actively leading our meetings, so we now had more structure than in the past. The meetings were still a highlight of our week, and had become very special to all of us. When our family moved away from San Diego and left Los Niños in 1978, it was the Mother's Group that I missed most of all. Years later when we visited San Diego one summer I went back to visit Los Niños. One of the mothers from our group was still there and was working as an assistant teacher. When she saw me, she ran up and gave me a hug, saying that I had meant more to her in those dark days than I had ever known. She said that I had been so strong, that I faced every problem with such calmness and control, and had been such a wonderful example for her. She knew that if I could do it, she could too! She had gone through a crushing divorce, but had managed to find hope and positiveness in her life, and was now in a very happy place. I had no idea that I had been a positive influence or had any impact whatsoever on others; at the time it seemed as if I was just struggling to get through myself, but now knowing I had helped her made me cry.

Cindy –
    You helped me so much
in the beginning – accepting Tiffany's
disability. You probably didn't realize
what a positive effect you had on
me but I thank you for being
there – and caring.
    Tiffany is still at Los Niños
& doing great!
                always –
                    Marti

Los Niños Education Center
6145 Decena Dr.
San Diego, CA 92120

THESE CARDS WERE DESIGNED BY PRESCHOOL-
AGED CHILDREN AT LOS NINOS REMEDIAL CENTER.
ADDITIONAL INFORMATION MAY BE OBTAINED
THROUGH VISTA HILL PSYCHIATRIC FOUNDATION,
7850 VISTA HILL AVENUE, SAN DIEGO, 92123.

*Cards*

# VOLUNTEERING — MY THERAPY

I was born into a family as the oldest of six children, with the youngest being 12 years younger. Therefore, I learned very early the values of "giving" and "helping". When my youngest sister was born, my mother was in the hospital for a week and the 14-year-old neighbor girl, Mary Ellen and I took care of the family during the day while my father was at work. My brother, the youngest child at home at the time, was two-years-old, so he was still in diapers and required help with daily activities. Mary Ellen and I did everything to run the household; cleaning, cooking, laundry, dishwashing and caring for the two-year-old. All the children in my large family had to learn to share, not only in the household tasks, but also our toys and other belongings. In addition we learned how to be compassionate to others, both at home and in the larger neighborhood and school settings.

We also grew up in an era when families were ashamed of relatives who were disabled, particularly if the disability was a mental condition. Medical knowledge about many such conditions was not very advanced, and there was much misunderstanding about the causes of many disabilities such as retardation and mental illness. It was believed that many of these disorders were genetic, and therefore they were not discussed because it would somehow blemish the family. If a family member suffered from a mental disability, the person was usually institutionalized and then ignored as if he/she didn't exist.

In our family, my Uncle Ted, my mother's brother, had a child, Susan, who was born with hydrocephaly, which is a condition that results in too much fluid on the brain and causes severe mental and nerve disorders. This was the late 1940's; Susan was placed in an institution shortly after birth, and was never discussed again by anyone in the family. I overheard some whispered conversations about her once and asked my mother about it, but was told that we "didn't discuss Susan, and especially not around Uncle Ted."

He was a physician, and I discovered many years later, after we learned about Steven's disorder, that Uncle Ted wanted to talk about Susan. He and I had a long conversation in which he told me all about her. He loved her, visited her often, but had needed to put her in a place where she could be cared for around the clock due to medical needs and the lack of any other options back in those days. Uncle Ted and Susan are now both gone, but I will always treasure that conversation I was able to have with Ted about our special needs children.

When I graduated from high school in 1959 and it was time to go to college, I gave very careful consideration to my career selection. Choices for women were much more limited in those days, but I really did not enjoy math and science so I was happy to consider the "helping" professions that were available at the time. I always loved children, but was most comfortable interacting with them individually or in small groups. Teaching a classroom of 25 to 30 children seemed to me like a daunting task, and not something that would be very enjoyable. The nursing profession was interesting, but I found it depressing to be around sick people too much, so decided to opt out of that as well. I decided that social work was really what I wanted to do. I realized that I had been very blessed to grow up with all of the privileges I had enjoyed, and that there were many people who were much less fortunate than I. So I decided I would like to "give back" and help others as much as I could through a career as a social worker.

After graduation from college, I obtained my first "real job" in my chosen profession as a social caseworker for the San Diego County Department of Public Welfare. I spent two years in this position, but it was a high "burnout" job. I was working in the poverty-stricken inner city with a caseload of the maximum allowed under Federal law, 65 families and there were no restrictions against being assigned additional cases from uncovered caseloads on an emergency basis. The problem was that the "emergency" was continuous, so the caseload was usually more than 65 and far too many cases for one caseworker. The result was a constant sense of frustration over never being able to feel effective or successful.

After two years I decided to go to graduate school to obtain a Masters degree in Social Work (MSW) so that I could work with children in either Child Protective Services or Adoptions. By this time I was married, and Phil was very supportive of my plans. Just prior to being accepted into graduate school, San Diego County offered me the job of my dreams as an adoptions caseworker without the requirement for the advanced degree. I loved my job, it was very fulfilling and rewarding, but after working two more years Phil and I wanted to start our own family, so I quit and became a "stay-at-home mom".

Mark and Steven were born in fairly quick succession, 19 months apart. I had considered in the back of my mind that I might return to work someday when the children were older and both in school, but once Steven started to exhibit first his severe physical problems, and then autism, this notion was forever removed from the realm of possibility. After Steven was officially diagnosed at UCLA, I no longer held any hope that he would ever be normal. At first I was devastated by the diagnosis; the denial was gone, but self-pity took over and I struggled with that for a long time. I kept asking myself "Why?" "Why had this happened to us?" "What had I done to deserve this worst possible of any fate that I could imagine?" I became really depressed. I cried anytime I was alone. I dreamed at night that all of a sudden Steven started talking and that he was normal after all; then I would wake up and realize it was a dream and I had to face another day. I felt like I was in a deep dark tunnel from which I would never emerge. All that existed in my world was the sorrow; I went through the motions of daily living, but I have no recollection of what was really going on outside of my own private darkness.

Eventually I started to emerge, realizing that there was no reason that I should be spared unhappiness in life. I asked myself then, "Am I so good that nothing bad should ever happen to me?" And of course I realized that the answer was "no", that bad things

51

happened to everyone, just as good things also happened in our lives. Awakening from the depression actually happened quite suddenly. One morning I woke up and realized that I needed to quit crying; that crying and being sad was not helping Steven, it was not helping me, and it certainly was not helping Steven's brother, Mark, or Phil, both of whom who really needed me too. As devastating as the diagnosis had been, it at least gave us a starting point, a place that we could begin to learn strategies for change and improvement. I knew that we had a big job ahead of us, and that I needed to focus my energy on doing positive things to improve all of our lives instead of feeling sad all of the time. So this was the beginning of the journey towards recovery for me and our family.

I have since learned that the denial followed by sadness and depression is a normal process for families facing similar circumstances. We are actually going through the steps of mourning, just as one mourns the death of a loved one. In a way it is a death for our families, because the child we thought we had is gone, as are the hopes and dreams we had for this child. Instead of planning a happy life for a normal child, we are facing huge unknowns, with multiple problems and unpredictable outcomes. I believe that if the family members are unable to go through the process of mourning, then it is much more difficult for them to face the reality of their situation and effectively cope with it.

After deciding that we could and must move forward with our lives, I immersed myself in information about autism. I read everything I could get my hands on, from articles in medical journals, to books and stories about other families and their autistic children. I joined the National Society for Autistic Children (NSAC) and went to my first autism convention in June, 1975. The convention was being held in San Diego where Dr. Bernard Rimland lived. He was a parent of an autistic adult, and also the founder and President of NSAC. Dr. Elizabeth M., our beloved director of Los Niños, was presenting a session on teaching methods and Dr. Ivar Lovaas was also a presenter along with other well known experts in the field of autism. For me, being able to attend this convention was a significant turning point in my healing process. I tried to absorb every word from every session, and to apply each idea to our child, hoping that helpful answers would be forthcoming. I was especially interested in the sessions that included adult autistic people with their parents, and found them to be so encouraging. Watching them gave me a sense of hope that a normal life would one day be possible for our family; that Steven could improve, and although he would never be normal, he could still live a fulfilling life, as could the rest of us. At the end of the conference I was exhausted, but I felt that I had found hope to go forward, something I sorely needed at that point.

The Los Niños Center was partially funded by the California State Regional Center for people with disabilities, and Steven was eligible for these services so he had a caseworker. In discussions with his caseworker, she learned that I also had a casework background, and wanted to know if I would serve on the San Diego Regional Center Training Committee. The purpose of the Training Committee was to find and distribute educational materials about developmental disabilities, including autism, to parents and professionals who were involved in caring for the needs of this population. I told her that I was learning about autism myself but that I would be happy to serve in any capacity that might be helpful; and I became the parent representative on this committee. Shortly before we left San Diego, I was also asked if I would fill a position on the board of the San Diego chapter of NSAC, which I gladly accepted. In addition, I was very involved with our own Mother's Group at Los Niños. There was no longer any time or need to feel depressed. I was filled with new energy and a renewed sense of hope. Volunteering to help others had become my therapy and I will be forever grateful that I was able to give of myself and heal from within at this critical time in our lives.

# FAMILY TIME

In the period of time when Steven was so ill, and later when we discovered that he was autistic, our family life was in shambles. Not only was autism destroying our marriage, it also was stealing Mark's childhood. As overwhelming as daily life was for me, it was ten times more so for Mark. It was extremely difficult for the adults to understand and cope with what was happening to us, but for Mark it had to be like a tornado going through his life and striking him down. Even now I can't begin to imagine what it was like for him. One minute he had two loving and caring parents, and the next everyone around him was frantic just trying to do the normal daily activities of living such as going to the store, eating meals, sleeping at night, and playing during the day. All of these normal activities were stolen from him and replaced by chaos.

If there was anything I could possibly change, it would have been providing protection for Mark from this life storm. And if there is any advice I can give to other parents, it is to spend time each and every day individually with your normal children. They need you as much, if not more than the disabled child.

Grandma was the saving grace for Mark and for us. She helped me take care of Mark when Steven was born, then she took care of the children when Mark was two years old, Steven was a baby, and Phil and I went to Europe for a vacation. And she spent weeks with us caring for Mark when Steven was so sick in the hospital. Grandma was Mark's substitute for me, the mother figure that I was unable to be for him during so much of his time in those early years. But Grandma lived over 1,000 miles from us in Denver and she had her own life there, so she was not available during the worst years of our learning how to remedy Steven's behavior.

When things were at their worst, Phil was working 24/7. We rarely saw him, and when he did come home he was exhausted as was I. He ate dinner then fell asleep in front of the TV. In the meantime, I had no chance to interact with him anyway, until after the children were in bed, and by that time I was ready to collapse. After we spent some time in marriage counseling, we both realized that this needed to change. I finally approached Phil in a rare quiet moment, and explained to him that I understood he was working very hard, and that he was stressed out about how much he had to do each day, but that we absolutely needed some family time together with him. He readily agreed, and asked what I would suggest, so I told him that I wanted Sundays to be "sacred" time for our family. Whatever work he was doing on Sunday could wait until Monday, and nothing should be more important to us than the children. He agreed, and Sunday became "Family Day" for as long as the children were living at home with us.

The next part of the solution to the problem was more difficult; deciding what activities we could do as a family that didn't put too much stress on us because of Steven's behavior. It was apparent that outdoor activities were easier than those indoors, especially in the beginning when Steven had not yet learned that throwing a temper tantrum was not going to be successful for him. Eventually we found activities that would be fun for everyone. A favorite was going to the San Diego Zoo.

Both children loved the Zoo, Mark for the animals, and Steven for the waterfalls. Later we were able to utilize the zoo as a learning experience for Steven too. When he learned to count, we asked him to count the animals in the cage as we looked at them. Later we asked him to tell us what color the animals were, and finally he was able to identify the names of many of the animals we looked at.

On one occasion when I was 8 ½ months pregnant with Geoffrey, our third child, we took a Sunday afternoon family outing to the San Diego Zoo. After several hours I was flagging, but the kids and Phil weren't ready to quit. Mark wanted to go see the monkeys, which were on the opposite side of the zoo from where we were, so I suggested that I would rest on the bench while Phil took Mark and Steven to see monkeys. I looked at my watch so that I would know approximately when to expect them back. It was a beautiful day, so I enjoyed just sitting on the bench watching the zoo visitors passing by. After a while I looked at my watch again, and decided that they would be back shortly. Phil knew I was tired and I didn't think he would leave me sitting there for too long. More time passed and pretty soon I started to feel uneasy about how long they had been gone. Way too much time had passed, and I was trying to decide if I needed to ask for help in finding them, when finally they appeared coming down the walkway towards me. Everyone except Steven was looking a little sheepish, so I said, "Okay what happened? Did Steven get into an animal cage or did he get hit by one of the tour buses?"

I was just kidding, I didn't think either one of those things had really happened; I was more inclined to think that they had just lost track of the time. Well, Mark's eyes got as big as saucers and he said, "How did you know?" He had been instructed by Dad not to tell Mom because it would really upset her. So then the truth came out – Steven HAD climbed into an animal cage!!!

Here is the rest of the story in Dad's own words:

*"Since Cindy was tired she decided to wait near the exit while I took Mark and Steven to see the Southeast Asia exhibit. There was a waterfall that fed a creek which meandered through the exhibit. Apparently, Steven needed to know where the water that fed the waterfall was coming from. Somehow, he slipped away from us and managed to get into the enclosure behind the waterfall. He climbed up on something that looked like a rock against the wall that was the apparent source of the waterfall. It was not a rock. It was the South American Tapir that lived in the exhibit. Just as I started to jump over the railing and the moat to get Steven, the rather large animal stood up, scaring Steven enough that he ran over to me. I was also getting verbal assistance from a busload of visitors that happened to be driving by."*

We have been forever grateful that it wasn't the lion cage that Steven decided to enter! Shortly after that incident we purchased a child harness that was worn by Steven thereafter on our outings.

Another favorite activity was going to Sea World; where Mark enjoyed viewing the fish and marine animals, while again Steven's main interest was the water. Once more we persevered and eventually Steven was counting the fish and telling us what color they were.

Since we lived on the beach, going there became a wonderful outing for everyone. There were tide pools on our beach, and Mark collected seashells, and was fascinated by the sea life he found in the tide pools. Steven could run around freely and splash in the water under Phil's watchful eye. I am a non-swimmer, but Phil as a former Navy SEAL was a professional in the water. Since Steven was drawn to water like a bee to honey, learning to swim was an important skill for both of our children. I had conscientiously taken both children for swimming lessons at the YMCA, but neither of them really mastered it until they went swimming with Phil. We joined a local recreational club that had a swimming pool, and going there became another activity we could do with them.

As Steven's behavior improved we were able to expand the activities that were available to us, and to enjoy each other. So once more, I can't stress enough the importance of time together as a family, especially for families with special needs children.

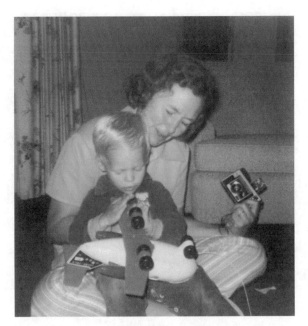

*Grandma taking care of Mark.*

*Dad teaching Steven to swim.*

*Steven riding a tricycle.*

*Mark, Mom and Steven at the zoo.*

*Steven and Mark at bedtime.*

# THE NEW BABY

By the time Steven was six years old and had been at Los Niños for 2 ½ years we had seen enormous progress, and felt that most of his behavior problems were under control, so Phil and I began to assess the possibility of having another child. We felt that the family dynamics would be more balanced if Mark had a non-disabled sibling and that his world growing up would be more normal. Thus, I became pregnant with our third child. By this time I was 35 years old, and was eligible for a genetic testing program which I gladly agreed to participate in. It was part of a grant program being conducted by UC San Diego Medical School, and an amniocentesis was performed as part of the experiment. When the results were returned they showed that the baby had a broken fourth chromosome, something that they had never seen before, and they were unable to give us any idea about what it meant for the baby. We were offered the option of an abortion, as they felt it could mean that the baby would be horribly deformed and/or damaged. However, they wanted to test the rest of the family first to see if any of us also had this "defect". This involved taking blood draws from the arms of each of us. Mark bravely held out his little arm for the test. Then it was Steven's turn and he was terrified of any medical procedures. He started to object strenuously, and a very concerned little Mark turned to Steven and said, "It will be okay, Steven, we have to do this, don't you want to have a little brother?" (We knew the baby was a boy at this point).

It was heart warming and a revelation to me that Mark really wanted to have his new baby brother. I knew at that moment that Phil and I had made the correct decision to try to have another child. As it turned out, Phil, Mark and Steven all had normal genotypes, but I also had the broken fourth chromosome. The doctor was then able to offer us the reassurance that this anomaly probably had no significance; that since I was normal, the baby would probably not be affected by it either.

Geoffrey joined our family in September, 1977 on Labor Day

weekend. My delivery took longer than anticipated so the doctor took some measures to speed things up. Then when Geoff was delivered he apparently swallowed some amniotic fluid and was having difficulty breathing. He was taken immediately to the intensive care unit of Children's Hospital which was adjacent to the hospital where I had delivered. I was having a tubal ligation procedure, so I was sedated right after delivery and had not seen the baby.

When I woke up in the recovery room, I was informed that my baby was in intensive care, and that I could not see him right away. Phil had gone to pick up my Mom at the airport, since she was coming to help us at home. When he returned to the hospital with Mom, he also was told that there was a problem and that it would be a little while before he could see the baby. Needless to say, we were all beside ourselves and in disbelief that something could be seriously wrong with this baby too. The doctors did try to reassure us that they didn't think there was any permanent damage, but that the baby needed to be in an oxygen tent for awhile. They told us that they were treating him for pneumonia, and that he was responding well.

As soon as I could be up and about I was taken in a wheelchair to the ICU and allowed to see and touch the baby. Phil was also allowed to be there. After 24 hours the oxygen was removed and the baby was brought to me for feedings, but he had to remain in the ICU for three days. Then he developed a high Billy Reuben reading (jaundice), and had to stay in the hospital another week after I had gone home. So we were commuting to the hospital daily to visit with our newborn; not exactly the way we had pictured welcoming this new little one into our family. Thankfully, he recovered, we took him home with us, and it appeared that the doctors had been correct, there were no longterm effects from this traumatic delivery and birth.

Geoffrey grew and developed normally and turned into an adorable chubby little toddler. Like Mark, he was intelligent and precocious, and it was so much fun to watch him grow and develop.

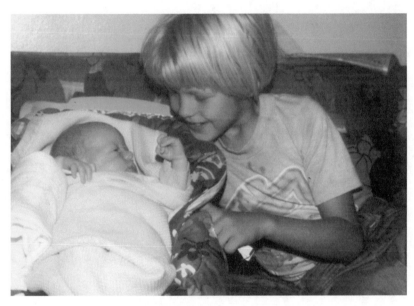

*Mark welcoming baby Geoff.*

# PART II

## THE MIDDLE YEARS

# MOVING TO WASHINGTON

We stayed one more year in California following Geoffrey's arrival, but our concern about the public schools, as well as the high property taxes, were causing us to start thinking about where we wanted to live to raise our family. Phil could take his building contractor skills just about anyplace and support the family. So we started to consider the qualities that we wanted to find in the community we would choose to live in. We wanted a more rural environment where crime would not be much of an issue, and where the children would have room to run and play outside. We were bothered by the smog in Southern California, and wanted to find someplace that had fresh air. We loved the climate in San Diego, and knew that it would be difficult to duplicate, but we wanted to find a place that had mild weather, not too cold in winter and not too hot in summer. We both loved the water (almost as much as Steven) and wanted to be someplace where there was boating and other water sports. We also enjoyed hiking and mountains, and wanted to have the availability of outdoor activities nearby. Of major importance to us was the quality of schools and affordable educational options. We needed to know that a program for Steven would be available, but we also wanted to make sure that our other two children would have a quality education.

We put our house in California on the market for sale, and sold it in a very short time for a very good price.

My sister, Joan and her family were living in Poulsbo, Washington at the time; and after we sold the house, she invited us to come and visit thinking that their community might be perfect for our family. We left San Diego to drive north on Thanksgiving weekend, and it took us six hours just to get through LA. We decided that was reason enough to leave Southern California, and it made us even more determined to find a place with a good quality of life. Poulsbo was perfect. It was located on a saltwater bay against the backdrop of the Olympic Mountain Range. It was a small town with a population of less than 5,000 people at the time. It was originally settled by Norwegian fishermen and has

67

retained its Norwegian character, with numerous small shops and restaurants, all with a Norwegian motif. We had contacted a local Realtor before leaving home, and he graciously spent a good part of his weekend showing us properties for sale.

We actually found a property that weekend and made an offer to purchase it. It was a six acre parcel on the waterfront, wooded and private, yet close to town and services. We returned for a second trip to make sure that this was what we wanted to do, and I researched the school situation on this trip. My sister was happy with the public schools in the community, so we decided to give them a try for Mark; but we didn't know much about the Special Education program and whether or not it would meet Steven's needs. So I made an appointment to visit the program that Steven would be enrolled in if we moved here. The classroom was a mixture of children with various types of developmental disabilities, but none of them had autism. The autistic child usually requires a highly structured environment with an abundance of "one-to-one" teaching time, so I was a little concerned about how Steven would adjust to this larger classroom with less individual time and attention. However, I knew that he had made excellent progress over the last two to three years at Los Niños, and that he might not require such intense therapy anymore. It would be a step forward if he were able to continue to learn in this larger and more unstructured classroom, so we were willing to take a chance on having it work for him. I talked to the teacher at length, asking her many questions about the types of children she had experience with, and about the materials that were used in the classroom. I came away with a very good feeling about Steven's chances of success in this school and with this teacher.

Many years later when I was still heavily involved in the schools in the community and was on the School Board, I ran into this teacher at a meeting. By that time Steven had exited the school system and was now in the job market, successfully holding down a job. I wanted to tell this teacher how much we appreciated her dedication and hard work with these very challenging children. She said that it was a joint effort between parents and

68

teachers, and that she appreciated my involvement as well. Then she laughed and told me that I was the only parent who had ever interviewed her before placing my child in her classroom.

We needed to make several trips between California and Washington in order to finalize the sale on our lot purchase. Several of the times we made the trek, the weather was typical Washington winter, with cloudy skies and drizzly rain. On a clear day the views were spectacular of the two mountain ranges that sandwich Puget Sound; the Cascades to the east and the Olympics to the west. On the first trip we made when the weather was clear, Steven looked up as we were driving down the highway, got an excited expression on his face and gleefully exclaimed "Ice Peem" as he looked up at the snowcapped mountains. He loved ice cream, and probably thought he had died and gone to heaven when he saw that huge amount of "ice cream" out of the window.

We purchased the property in Poulsbo in November, 1977, two months after Geoffrey was born. Phil had business to complete in California, I didn't want to take Mark out of school in the middle of the year, and I also wanted to keep Steven in Los Niños as long as possible, so we moved out of the home we had sold and moved first into a rental condo, then into a temporary interim home we had purchased until we were ready to make the physical move north. On our last trip to Washington before moving there, we found a little farmhouse to rent while we built our new home. The farmhouse was about half a mile from my sister and her family. Phil was still building a house in Mammoth Lakes California, on a property that we owned, and so a decision was made for me to take the children to Washington in time to enroll them in school for the Fall. Phil would follow us as soon as he finished the house, estimated to be early January. It was very nice for me to be near my sister, Joan, since I was new to the area, and very much alone until Phil arrived. She was wonderful; took me under her wing, introduced me to her friends, and included our family as much as possible in events and outings that her family was involved in.

*Steven's mountains with "Ice Peem"*

# SCHOOL ENROLLMENT

After settling into the farmhouse, the next order of business was getting Mark and Steven enrolled in school. The school Mark would attend once we moved into the new home that we would build was in a different geographic area than the school he would have attended while living in the farmhouse. Once more, I was concerned about disruptions to his life, not wanting to make him change schools mid-year, so I needed to convince the school administration to let me enroll him in Suquamish Elementary, the school he would attend when we moved to our permanent location. They were amenable as long as I provided the transportation for him from home to school, about a 10 mile drive, which I gladly agreed to do. As it turned out, this became a very positive experience for Mark, because I had daily contact with the teacher when picking him up after school. His teacher was one of those special people whom you remember for a lifetime because they are so sincerely dedicated to teaching the children in their classrooms. Any time she had questions or concerns I was readily available to discuss them, and we also got positive feedback from her on all of his successes.

Enrolling Steven was also an adventure. There was no question that he would need Special Ed services, but the school district needed to do extensive testing to determine what services they would be able to offer him. They would not be able to give him the one-to-one personal attention he had been receiving at Los Niños; but they did have significant classroom support, with very small class sizes and several teaching assistants all day. They also used many of the same teaching materials that Steven was familiar with from Los Niños.

One of the first questions I asked was, "What about a summer program? Is this offered?" I was told that this was not available, and I expressed some consternation about this void in services. I explained that for autistic children, the year round consistent program with no large breaks was really important for overall functioning. I had visions of having to start a program myself for Steven in the summer, but I also had two other children who needed summer activities and felt stressed about finding the time for all of it. I talked to Dr. Ann L., the school psychologist about all of this, and she listened carefully. Finally, she told me that another mother who had just moved from California was also quite concerned about this lack of a summer program. Her child had Down's Syndrome, and also required a lot of structured activities to maximize his learning. Ann suggested that perhaps we could schedule a meeting for the three of us to discuss possibilities of starting a program.

We arranged an evening meeting and at the appointed time Jean W. arrived, knitting in hand, to join Ann and me in the living room of the farmhouse to discuss the all-important creation of a summer program for the special needs children in the North Kitsap School district. The three of us brainstormed about a potential program; we had only nine months to work out all of the details, so we needed to get started right away.

Ann immediately involved the Special Ed Director Dr. Ron S., who was very supportive of the idea and more than happy to help us. He said that we would be able to use District facilities and teaching materials, and he would also help us procure the staff and put them on District payroll, but we would have to figure out a way to fund the staff. Since many teachers actively look for summer employment, he didn't think it would be much of a problem to secure the staff.

We were thrilled, as the District was really offering to do the lion's share of the work for us. So we enthusiastically jumped into the fund-raising project. First we needed to establish an official parents' organization to sponsor our program, and so the Learning Center PTA was formed for parents and staff involved with the Special Education Program in our school district.

At our early meetings we met with the parents and staff to brainstorm some more about fundraising possibilities. At the time, there were no hot lunch programs in the schools, so one of our ideas was to provide a hot lunch one day a week that we would sell to raise money. The Special Ed program was housed in Poulsbo Elementary, and the Principal was totally supportive of our plan to sell a hot lunch in his school. The school had a basic kitchen but we needed to choose a menu that we could start cooking in the morning and have ready for multiple students by noon. We decided on hot dogs, chips, pop, and a cookie. We then approached the local supermarket, explained to the owner what we were doing, and asked if he could give us a price break for bulk buying. He was more than happy to accommodate that request, so we were up and running in a few short weeks. The parents volunteered their time to do the purchasing, set up and cooking, and selling on hot lunch day. I did the bookkeeping since I had experience from keeping the books for Phil's contracting business. In today's world the menu we chose would have been considered an unhealthy option, but the children were very excited about having a hot lunch one day a week, even if it was hot dogs. Parents also were happy to have one day a week that they didn't need to pack a cold lunch, and so we were able to raise the funds for the summer program our special needs children so desperately needed.

By the time summer arrived, we were "ready to roll" with our summer program. It was a huge success, loved by all – parents, children and staff. The regular teacher who received the children back in the fall was also delighted by the retention of skills over the summer. This program remained in place until Steven "graduated" from the public school, and by that time it was being funded by the State, with summer programs becoming mandatory statewide. We do not claim credit for the statewide changes; most likely they would have happened anyway, but we did plant a seed in our own district and it grew successfully.

# FIRST WASHINGTON WINTER

Our introduction to winter in Washington was "baptism by fire". We knew it rained a lot, both by reputation and personal observation. Our first trip north had been at Thanksgiving the year before, and it rained the entire week we were there looking for property to purchase; but I hadn't expected the totally rainy Fall that we had experienced our first year of living there. The weather really was dismal; cloudy and overcast every single day. After helping us get moved and settled into the farmhouse, Phil returned to California to finish his construction project of the vacation ski home in Mammoth Lakes, so I was on my own with the children, getting them started in school and adjusting to our new life.

When Phil came to Washington for the Thanksgiving holiday, Geoffrey was 14 months old and just learning to walk. He toddled around but was still very unsteady on his feet. There was a large furnace vent in the living room of the farmhouse that was covered by a removable grate. Steven was always curious about everything, and had no trouble removing the grate to see what was down there. Since it was a large open hole going directly down to the concrete floor of the unfinished basement where the large oil furnace was housed, I decided to locate the sofa over the top of the vent so that Steven could not remove the grate. Then Phil arrived not knowing about the problem and decided to move the sofa so that it was located more directly in front of the TV. I was unaware that he had moved things around, and from another part of the house I suddenly heard piercing screams from the direction of the living room. Phil and I both rushed to the room at the same time to discover that Steven had removed the grate and Geoffrey had toddled into the hole and fallen to the concrete floor below. For a second we were frozen in fear; then Phil jumped into action and ran below to rescue Geoff. Fortunately, the furnace was not running at the time, and Geoffrey had landed on his feet, not his head. We rushed him to the doctor's office and learned that he had a fracture in one leg, but fortunately no other injuries. We were told that there was nothing that could be done for the fracture except to keep him off of it as much as possible until it had time to heal. What I learned from this is that I not only had to protect Steven from his own age-inappropriate behaviors, but I also had to protect the baby from the consequences of some of those behaviors.

Even though my sister and her husband were nearby, I felt nervous about being alone with the children in the farmhouse. When Phil and I were just married and had our first house at the beach, we got a puppy, a little female "Heinz 57" that became our "first child". We both loved the dog, but after Steven was born, our small two-bedroom, 600-square foot house was way too small for two children, two adults and a dog. My mother graciously gave the dog a home with her in Denver, and until now we had not considered getting another one. But at this time, I was seriously thinking about getting a dog now rather than waiting until our new house was built. Phil and I had discussed getting a Black Labrador Retriever as our next family dog, so I started watching the ads in the local newspaper and located a litter of puppies for sale. Of course I fell in love with the puppies the moment I saw them, and selected the largest and most active puppy in the litter, a male that we named "Max". All three of the children were delighted with having Max as an addition to our family, but Steven's relationship to Max was especially interesting. Max as a puppy was only interested in playing with the children, but in subsequent years he developed a special attachment to Steven and became quite protective, apparently by instinct and without any special training.

Shortly after the first of the year in 1979, Phil joined us permanently in Washington. The family that had rented their farmhouse to us were unable to stay at the place they had moved because of complications in their job situation, so shortly after Phil arrived, we had to move again to a different rental house while he built our new home on the property we had purchased.

76

Shortly after moving into the new rental we experienced one of the fiercest winter storms that had hit western Washington in over 30 years. I was so fortunate that Phil was in Poulsbo. The wind started blowing in the middle of the night and by daybreak it was howling. Our house was surrounded by very tall fir trees with thin trunks, and as we watched out of the windows, we saw the trees falling down like matchsticks. The power had gone out hours earlier, so we were awake listening to the battery-powered radio as the announcer was giving report after report of major damage, and talking about wind speeds of over 75 mph. Most of western Washington was without power at this point, and the wind did not seem to be abating. Then we heard the announcer say, "Wait a minute, we just got a report, it must be a joke, I don't believe it" followed by a long silence. Then, "Yes, folks, it IS true, the Hood Canal Bridge just blew down."!! We were stunned; this bridge is a floating bridge over two miles long which linked the Kitsap Peninsula, where we lived, to the Olympic Peninsula, where we often went for drives to the mountains or longer drives to the ocean. Fortunately, due to the hour of the day and the ferocity of the storm that had kept people inside, there were no cars on the bridge when it went down. It took about three years to rebuild the bridge, and in the meantime people going to the Olympic Penin-sula either had to make a three hour drive around, or wait in line sometimes for several hours to ride on the small temporary car ferry that the state put in place while a new bridge was built.

One of the lessons we learned from this is that power outages were common in our new home because there is so much rain and so many trees, and whenever there was a windstorm, trees would inevitably fall on power lines someplace. In the case of this storm, it was many days until power was restored, and I was grateful that Phil was there to help in the shared responsibility of keeping the children warm and fed without any power for heat or cooking.

# THE NEW SCHOOL

For the most part, Steven's adjustment to the public school setting went very smoothly. While he did not get the intense one-to-one ratio of instructors and helpers, the class was small enough that he did receive as much special attention as was necessary for him to continue to develop his skills. The public school was interested in mainstreaming the Special Ed students into the regular classrooms as much as possible, and they had developed an excellent program to facilitate this process. Regular classes were selected to fit the student's abilities, such as Phys Ed; and art and music classes. This gave the children in Special Ed the experience of interacting with the non-disabled children in a normal setting. This kind of socialization was particularly important for Steven, because he needed to have role models to imitate in order to learn appropriate ways of interacting normally in everyday situations. The students in the regular classrooms were prepared for the entrance of the Special Ed students by teaching them to be empathetic and enlisting their help as part of a team with the teacher to include the Special Ed students in classroom activities.

It was mandated by law for the schools to provide transportation services for the Special Ed students appropriate to their special needs. This meant that the school district had to hire special drivers who used their personal vehicles to transport the students. There were two drivers for Steven's class, one who drove a red van, and the other who drove a blue van. Steven described his drivers to us as "Red Rena" and "Blue Dot". Rena and Dot did not have any special training in the behavior management of these special needs children, and inevitably there were behavior issues while riding in the vans back and forth from school.

The school district had to meet the legal requirement of drawing up very specific goals and behavior management plans for each child, called the Individual Educational Plan or IEP. Conferences were held with the parents and everyone signed off on the plan. If there were problems in the implementation of the IEP, parents were consulted and changes were made if necessary. The one glaring gap in these plans, however; was the omission of a plan to deal with behavior problems during the commute for students in the Special Ed transportation program. About three or four months after the beginning of the school year, Steven started telling us that "Red Rena did spray the face".

At first we thought that we had misunderstood him, but when he became more and more agitated about riding with "Red Rena" we decided that we needed to ask some questions and find out what was happening. So I met the van after school one day and asked Rena if she knew what Steven was talking about. Well, the story came out; Rena had in fact been spraying Steven in the face. She told me that he was making too much noise while she was driving, so she took it upon herself to solve the problem by getting a spray bottle with vinegar in it and spraying it in his mouth when he was too loud. Needless to say, an immediate phone call was placed to the District office to discuss the discontinuation of this practice and to develop an alternative plan to address the unwanted behavior. It was also a "wake up" call for the District, helping them to realize that the special needs of these students did not stop at the classroom door, and that parents, teachers and drivers needed to develop plans for the transportation portion of the program as well as the classroom portion.

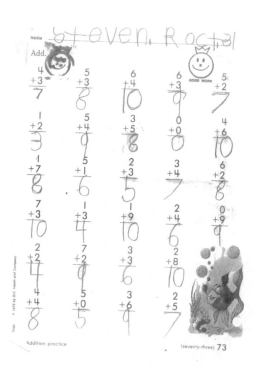

| | | | | |
|---|---|---|---|---|
| 4 +3 = 7 | 5 +3 = 8 | 6 +4 = 10 | 6 +3 = 9 | 5 +2 = 7 |
| 1 +2 = 3 | 5 +4 = 9 | 3 +5 = 8 | 0 +0 = 0 | 4 +6 = 10 |
| 1 +7 = 8 | 5 +1 = 6 | 2 +3 = 5 | 3 +4 = 7 | 6 +2 = 8 |
| 7 +3 = 10 | 1 +3 = 4 | 1 +9 = 10 | 2 +4 = 6 | 0 +9 = 9 |
| 2 +2 = 4 | 7 +2 = 9 | 3 +3 = 6 | 2 +8 = 10 | |
| 4 +4 = 8 | 5 +0 = 5 | 3 +6 = 9 | 2 +5 = 7 | |

Addition practice

(seventy-three) 73

Steven R Octec

| pad | ram |
|---|---|
| on | the |
| The | is |

The ram is on the pad.

| man | on |
|---|---|
| mat | The |
| the | is |

The man is on the mat.

| on | van |
|---|---|
| The | jam |
| is | the |

The jam is on the van.

15

*School work packet - Poulsbo Elementary: October 1980.*

81

July 31

Dear mom and Dad

Hi how are you? I am ~~having fun in summ~~ ... I am learning how to write letters and I wanted you to ... the first ones I wrote you to ... are the best mom and Dad anyone could have. I love you.

Love always
Steven R.

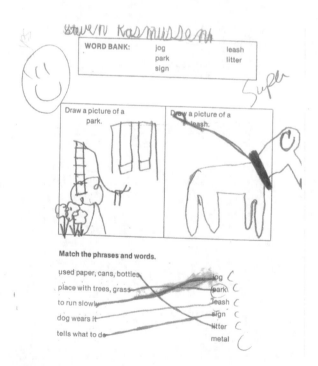

Steven Rasmussen

WORD BANK: jog    leash
park    litter
sign

Draw a picture of a park.    Draw a picture of a leash.

Match the phrases and words.

used paper, cans, bottles — jog
place with trees, grass — park
to run slowly — leash
dog wears it — sign
tells what to do — litter
metal

*School work packet - Poulsbo Elementary: January 1981.*

82

What time is it?

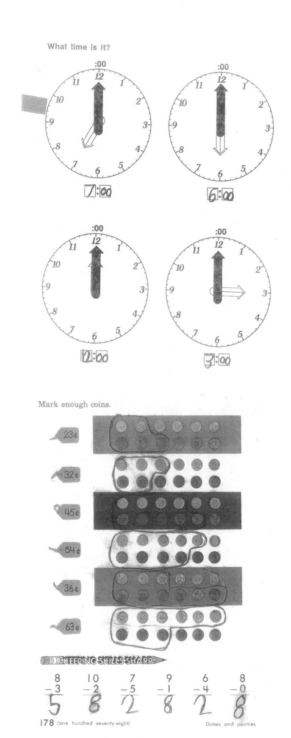

:00    :00

7:00    6:00

:00    :00

12:00    3:00

Mark enough coins.

23¢
32¢
45¢
54¢
36¢
63¢

KEEPING SKILLS SHARP

$$\begin{array}{cccccc} 8 & 10 & 7 & 9 & 6 & 8 \\ -3 & -2 & -5 & -1 & -4 & -0 \\ \hline 5 & 8 & 2 & 8 & 2 & 8 \end{array}$$

178 (one hundred seventy-eight)                    Dimes and pennies

*School work packet - Poulsbo Elementary: January 1981.*

83

# THE NEW HOME

Phil had started the permitting process for our new house as soon as he arrived in January, and by early spring he was well into the construction project. As the weather improved, I started taking the children to the site after school so we could visit with Phil, observe progress, and let the children run and play on our new property. It was six wooded acres with over three hundred feet of waterfront on a body of water called Agate Passage. The property was primarily high bank, but it did include a cut with a walking path to the pebble and gravel beach below. Much of the wooded area had been heavily overgrown with blackberries that had thick vines and nasty stickers. By the time we started construction much of this undergrowth had been cleared for the building pad, the driveway and the well and septic system, so a much larger area of the property was now usable.

One sunny Saturday afternoon, I took the children to the property to play and visit. Phil had a small crew present and was busy working with them, so I played with eighteen-month-old Geoffrey nearby while Mark, Steven, and Max the dog ran down the footpath to play at the water's edge. They came back about every 20 minutes to check in with us and Mark promised to keep an eye on Steven. We weren't really worried that they could get into any trouble, because they would have to travel past us to leave the property; the only place to go was the beach and back to the construction site. We knew that Steven was fascinated with water, but the water at the beach was very shallow for quite a distance from the beach and he was happy to play in the shallow area.

However, after about the third trip between the beach and the property, Mark and Max returned without Steven. Max was quite agitated and kept running back to the path to the beach, seemingly wanting us to follow him, so of course we did. Mark explained that he was just looking at some little fish in the water, and when he looked up Steven was gone. He thought Steven had come back to us. In minutes we had a search party consisting of about three guys from Phil's construction crew, Phil, Mark and myself. Several years earlier we had purchased an ID bracelet for Steven which he wore permanently. It had his name, phone number and address, plus it identified him as having autism. However, I had forgotten to get a new bracelet when we moved to Washington, plus I wanted it to have our permanent address and phone number instead of having to get a new one every time we moved. So his bracelet had the old California information, absolutely useless for the present situation.

After about 30 minutes of searching, we felt compelled to call law enforcement for help. We did not have a phone nearby, so I walked up to the local convenience store about ¼ mile up the road to use their payphone. I made the "missing child" report to the 911 operator, and was walking back to the property when a Sheriff's car drove toward me. I flagged him down to tell him about our problem, and after he listened to me for a few seconds, he pointed to the back seat and said, "Does he look familiar?" To my huge relief, there was Steven sitting in the back seat of the Sheriff's patrol car. He was not immediately released to me; I had to prove that I was his mother and answer some questions about what had happened, but in the end the Sheriff drove to our construction site, talked to everyone there, and left Steven with us.

### THE REST OF THE STORY

While Mark was preoccupied watching the small fish in the water, Steven had taken off down the beach. The homes to the north were located on low bank waterfront, with the front lawns reaching right down to the water's edge. There was a rather large lawn party at one of the homes which caught Steven's attention. This home had a dock with several small row boats on it, and Steven decided it would be fun to go for a little boat ride by himself. He managed to get in the boat and was drifting out into Agate Passage when someone at the party noticed him in the boat. That person asked some other guests if anyone recognized the kid in the boat, and of course no one did, so an adult got in another boat, went out and pulled Steven back to the dock. Coincidentally, one of the children at the party was David, a young boy who had Down's Syndrome, and the owners of the home were his grandparents. When David saw Steven get out of the boat, he said, "That's Steven, he's in my class at school."

One of the problems with autism is that on the surface these children appear to be so normal, and therefore people don't understand why their behavior is so bizarre. So David, in identifying Steven as being in his Special Ed class, provided a clue as to why a perfect stranger would get in their boat and take it out into the water unannounced and without permission. Someone then discovered Steven's ID bracelet, but since it had only the old California information on it, they did not know how to find us or call us to come and get him. Their only option was to call the Sheriff for help in trying to find out where Steven belonged. We never did find out what the procedure for the Sheriff's office would be, since we found Steven in the Deputy's squad car before it was implemented, but we do know that the Deputy was on the way to deliver Steven to a temporary foster home until we, the parents could be located.

Fortunately the story had a happy ending, but it easily could have ended in a tragedy, because Agate Passage is a very fast flowing body of water, and a small boat could easily be overturned, drowning the occupant in the very cold water. A normal eight year old would have been able to communicate to us his attraction to the boat and his desire to go out in it. He also would have known that he should not take the boat without the permission of the owner and his parents. Steven, however, was not able to communicate his desire to us and had no understanding of ownership of the boat, so when he saw that it was available and wanted to take it out for a ride, he just did it.

The problem for parents of autistic children is that these children continue to grow up and develop the same physical skills and abilities as other children their age, but they do not have the age-appropriate judgment to go along with the abilities. Furthermore, parents need to start granting more independence to all of their children as they grow and mature, including those with disabilities. But it is more difficult to determine the proper amount of independence to grant a child with autism due to the lack of communication skills, and it becomes a "learning by trial and error" experience for the parents. We couldn't and wouldn't keep Steven locked in the house or constantly on a "short leash" as he got older, so we tried to give him as much independence as seemed reasonable to us while still providing the cautionary oversight. We always thought he was safe at the times we let him go out of sight when he was with his older brother, but Mark was also yet a child, and if Steven was able to slip away quickly and unnoticed from us, it certainly was not fair to expect Mark to be a perfect watchdog either. So the possibility was always there that an accident could happen. We did, however, replace the ID bracelet post haste, and we also scolded Steven soundly, telling him he was NEVER, EVER to go in a boat again without having us with him. We are certain that he understood, because he never did this again, and later we were able to safely keep a small rowboat of our own down on our beach that he never touched without permission.

### SUMMER, 1979

By mid-summer we moved into our new home and our lives settled into a comfortable rhythm. The summer program that parents and staff had put together for our special needs children was in full swing and going very well. In fact the program was such a success that everyone enthusiastically supported the effort for years thereafter, until summer programs for Special Education students became mandated by law. Steven went to his summer school every morning, five days a week, for six weeks. I signed Mark up for other summer activities, and baby Geoff stayed home and played with me. Phil started several other construction projects, building one or two custom homes at a time. Often, in the afternoons I would take the children to visit Phil at the job sites, and Steven started learning how to "help Dad". He learned how to pound nails and turned out to be quite good at it.

He approached the job with a desire for exact accuracy, following Phil around and finding "missed nails". He was also very physically adept and strong, so we allowed him to climb on the ladders, helping to hold the other end of the boards, or carry the other end of the drywall sheets for Phil. He enjoyed being kept busy with new tasks and was able to learn anything that didn't involve social skills pretty quickly. He also started to develop a sense of pride in his accomplishments. He loved being at the construction sites, and seemed to find them stimulating and exciting, so Phil tried to involve him as much as possible whenever we were able to come by to visit. It didn't take long for construction sites to hold the same attraction for Steven as water and elevators.

The Suquamish Tribe owned the thirteen acres of property adjacent to ours, and they were in the process of building a large new Tribal Center during and after the construction of our home. Steven was as fascinated with the Tribal construction project as he was with his Dad's work sites, and he started visiting their site on his own. The work crews did not object to his presence, as he mainly just walked around and watched them, and he was always accompanied by Max, who had started following Steven everywhere.

Max had become quite protective of Steven but I didn't realize how protective until one day, after the Tribal Center was finished and people were moving in, a Tribal Member appeared at the front door requesting my assistance in removing Max and Steven from one of the offices. I had not realized that construction was complete and that they were moving in, so I had not restricted Steven's movements on their property. I was of course very apologetic, and went immediately to take care of the situation, but we had to smile at the circumstances. Steven was having a great time exploring the finished building, with Max trailing along. When someone had asked Steven to leave, he hadn't understood and Max got very protective, growling and not allowing anyone to even approach Steven. As soon as I arrived, Max wagged his tail and came right to me, as did Steven, and we had to now tell Steven the Tribal Center was "off limits".

*Steven with Max the dog.*

*Steven and Geoff playing in the back yard.*

*The new Washington house.*

*The Family in front.*

# These Olympians Are Special

Staff photos by John McCurdy

## ... And They Have Some Fun

Saturday's track and field competition in Kitsap's Special Olympics yielded some stellar performances, as well as its share of laughter and joy. Steve Rassmussen and Jenay Miles squared off in the 100-meter dash, above. But when they got to the finish line in a dead heat, both stopped at the tape and smiled at each other conspiratorily. Below, Jenay was finally coaxed across the finish line. Steve looked on in amusement. Both received first place ribbons, and a round of applause. Lower left, Raymond White was a runaway winner in the 400 meters.

*Bremerton Sun, summer 1982.*

# SPECIAL ABILITIES

Many autistic people have what are described as savant abilities, or a few isolated abilities that far exceed what a person with normal intelligence would be able to do; yet they remain significantly impaired in other aspects of functioning that are common to autism, such as language and socialization skills. Steven exhibited some of these savant abilities from an early age.

## SPACIAL CONCEPTS/PUZZLES

The earliest savant ability that Steven exhibited was being able to put together a complicated puzzle at two years of age. He had not yet been diagnosed as having autism, and I was carefully observing all of his behaviors in an effort to find out what was wrong and why he was not learning to talk. The most obvious conclusion that one might draw under those circumstances would be that he was mentally retarded; but I immediately ruled out that diagnosis when I observed him putting together puzzles that were far above his age level and doing it in jig time.

## ROUTE MEMORIZATION

Another savant skill was his uncanny ability to memorize a driving or walking route to places of interest to him after going there or being driven past only once.

At Christmas time in 1978, shortly after we had moved to Washington and before Phil had joined us, I flew with the children, ages nine, seven, and one, to California to spend Christmas at the new ski house in Mammoth Lakes with him. The house was almost completed, and he was planning to return to Washington with us shortly after Christmas, but we decided it would be fun for us to enjoy the new house a week or so during school Christmas vacation. Mammoth Lakes receives a lot of snow in the winter, and at least three to four feet of snow was on the ground when we arrived.

Phil picked us up at the airport in Reno and we drove to Mammoth. This resort town was quite small, but several large condominium projects had started to spring up and we passed them on the drive to our new cabin which was a few miles up the hill from the main part of town. Near the end of our stay it started snowing again, and this time it was a major storm, dropping three to five feet more snow on top of what was already there. The day we had planned to leave, we woke up to the news that we were snowed in; there was literally no way to get out of Mammoth Lakes until the snow stopped and some of the roads could be cleared. Phil had cleared a small path around the perimeter of the cabin and also a vehicle size path from the driveway to the road. The snow had stopped, but it also was up to the eaves of the roof, higher than all of the windows and doors.

Phil and I were sitting in the kitchen having coffee, when Mark asked if he and Steven could go outside and play in the snow. So we bundled them up and sent them out the door, not too worried about anything happening to them as the snow appeared to be too deep for them to go anywhere except around the path that Phil had cleared. They went out the back door, circled the cabin and came in the front door, Mark declaring that it was "really fun" to run around the cabin and they wanted to go again. After making the circle for about 15 or 20 minutes, Mark came in without Steven. We immediately asked Mark, "Where is Steven?", to which he replied that he didn't know.

We knew that Steven had the ability to disappear in the blink of an eye under normal conditions, but we didn't think he could get very far very quickly under present conditions, so we bundled up and went outside to look for him. It would have been impossible for him to go anyplace except back into the cabin or out to the road. The roads did have packed snow, but no traffic, and there was no way to go off of the road due to the deep snow, so we began a search up and down the road. At times back in San Diego, Steven had gone into neighboring homes searching for new and exciting water sources, so we checked with nearby neighbors to see if any of them had seen him. The result was negative, and after a half hour or so of searching on our own we decided it was time to call for professional help.

There was no phone in the new cabin, so we went to the nearest neighbor's house to call the Sheriff. The Sheriff responded immediately, requesting that I stay at the cabin in case Steven returned there on his own, and that Phil continue to look for him in his truck, covering a different direction than the Deputy. An hour or so went by, which seemed like an eternity for me, with no results. No one could find Steven within several miles of the cabin, and no one could imagine that he had gone any further than that under the snow conditions on the road and on the ground. After several hours, a Sheriff's Jeep appeared in the driveway, the Deputy got out, opened the back door and got Steven out of the vehicle wearing handcuffs. The handcuffs were way too big and Steven slipped out of them by himself. About the same time Phil drove up, and all of us breathed a sigh of relief to see Steven safely returned to us.

Our immediate question was, "Where did you find him?" It turned out that Steven, who was obsessed with elevators, had noted the condominiums when we had arrived driving through town that first time. He had taken note of the tall buildings, and correctly ascertained that they would have elevators. So at the first opportunity of "freedom" he made a beeline for the condos with the elevators. Shortly after we called the Sheriff about a missing autistic child, their office received a call from the front desk of one of the condos regarding a strange child who was riding up and down in the elevators over and over again. The Sheriff's office put two and two together, and brought Steven home to us.

As the Deputy was leaving, Phil asked, "By the way, why was he wearing handcuffs?" The Deputy's response, "He was having too much fun and didn't want to come with me." Since the story had a good ending, Phil and I still smile about seven-year-old Steven being returned to us with handcuffs because he was having too much fun playing with elevators and didn't want to come home. This was our first encounter with law enforcement regarding Steven, but there would be more such incidents in the years to come, and for many years, when we discussed with Steven that a policeman is your friend if you are lost, he would tell us that, "Policeman put handcuffs on you."\

## MECHANICAL ABILITY

As Steven grew a little older he also became much calmer most of the time. He was acquiring more and more language, and as he did so, his frustration level diminished considerably. He also developed a lot of curiosity about his surroundings, and was particularly interested in how things worked, especially electronic things. He tried to turn on anything that had a motor or moving parts, such as television sets, radio, VCR, dishwasher, washing machine and dryer. Inevitably, something would break and when that happened he became extremely agitated and upset, either because he was frustrated that he was unable to make it work, or because he knew that we would be upset with him for breaking it. In either case we needed to teach him the correct way to use things or train him to leave them alone. Since I was busy taking care of the house, the business, and three children, it was easier to teach him to leave things alone unless I was there to supervise.

However, I was not always successful. We had recently purchased a new VCR and placed it upstairs in the den. One day we went to use it, and found that it was broken. Steven was present, so we asked him if he had touched it. He immediately became upset saying, "No, no broken, Steven no broken". We tried to calm him down and tell him it was okay, we would fix it. We left the room and didn't return to it until several days later. My intent had been to take the VCR to the repair shop and see if it could be fixed before buying a new one. Well, I walked into the den and on the floor were the pieces of the VCR totally taken apart. Without thinking I said, "Oh no! Steven, did you do that?" Again he was upset and said, "Steven fix it, Steven fix it!" So I told him it was okay, we could get a new one.

Several days later we were again in the den, and to our amazement the VCR was put totally back together. Phil said, "Let's see if it works", but I thought to myself that he was being very unrealistic, there was no way that it would work now. Again, to my complete amazement, when we turned it on it worked perfectly! To this day we have no idea how Steven was able to take this complicated piece of electronics apart, fix it and put it back together again so that it worked; and he has never repeated this unbelievable skill.

## *CALENDAR CALCULATION AND EVENT MEMORY*

He did, however, begin to exhibit other skills and abilities, some of which were also pretty astounding to us when we discovered them. When he was younger and still attending the Los Niños Center, he began to learn basic math. He could add and subtract quite well, and even learned some basic multiplication. He continued to use and improve upon this skill when he entered the public school setting in Washington, and we noticed that he was starting to take great interest in calendars, especially as they applied to people's birthdays and special events that were planned ahead for him. One day he casually told us what day of the week his birthday would fall on in the following year. We were curious about whether or not he was correct, so we found a calendar for the next year, and sure enough, he had the correct day of the week for his birthday. We then wondered if he had simply seen a calendar for next year and paid attention to the one date that was important to him, so we asked him about some other dates of family birthdays, and unbelievably, he made a correct match for the day of the week of any future date that we asked him about.

We were then very curious about how much more date related information he was able to calculate, so we asked about dates in the past, and once more he was correct every time, including being able to calculate for Leap Years. We discovered that he could match dates with many activities other than birthdays, and that in fact, he had total recall for most dates that we asked him about, including what the weather had been on that date and what he had for meals.

At one point, many years later, we moved from our property near Poulsbo to a new home we built on the Olympic Peninsula as our retirement home. Phil and I built the home literally by ourselves except for contracting out the electrical, and some of the plumbing, and while we were building it, we also took numerous trips and vacations. It took us a total of two years to build the home starting from the date we received the building permit until the date we received the occupancy permit. Steven, age 35 years old at the time, was our helper and actually provided much of the heavy lifting labor for us throughout those two years. He had a job at this time, but he helped us on his days off. He loved the days he got to work on the new house. He was always very "tuned in" to our trips, as it meant that he wouldn't be able to work with us for awhile until we returned from our trip. It also meant that there were breaks in the progress of the construction job.

We were driving in the car one day many months after we had completed the new home, and were casually discussing what the length of time it had taken us to build that house. Steven was sitting in the back seat listening to our discussion, and all at once he started counting. We could not figure out why. We tried to interrupt him to ask what he was doing, but he was not to be deterred in his counting, and totally ignored our questioning, instead staying totally absorbed in his counting task. After about 20 minutes, he blurted out in triumph "557 days"!! It was then that we realized he had been calculating the total number of days that we had actually spent working on the house, starting with the day we broke ground until we got our final occupancy permit, and subtracting the days we had been on trips and had not done any work. It was and is amazing that he is able to do those kinds of calculations in his head and we have not been able to figure out how he does it, but it is almost always completely accurate.

# THE TEEN YEARS

We were so busy that the years slipped quickly by and before we knew it, Steven and Mark had become teenagers. The teenage years have their own set of challenges for parents and children, and autistic children are not immune from these "growing pains". However, we noticed some subtle but positive changes as Steven became a teenager. As he matured and developed greater language and communication skills, he became less dependent on rigid routines and "sameness" in his environment. He exhibited a lot more flexibility when changes in plans were necessary, and he also became more observant and aware of other people.

A humorous example of this took place when we were at Yellowstone National Park for a family reunion of my mother's side of the family in 1988. There were about 25 relatives taking part in this reunion, and we had gathered outside of Old Faithful Lodge one morning in order to make plans for the day. Needless to say, with that many people involved, there were lots of different ideas about what we should do. Steven stood there quietly listening and observing for awhile, then turned to my sister and said, "Joan, why is Steven laughing?"

Joan replied, "I don't know Steven, why are you laughing?" Steven's reply, "Nobody can decide."

At the same time as he started becoming aware of others, he also started paying more attention to things taking place around him in his environment. When he was younger he liked to watch Sesame Street and Mr. Rogers Neighborhood on TV. As a teenager, and finally as an adult, his awareness of the surrounding environment and events became even more apparent. When he was a young adult he started sitting down in the living room and watching the evening news with us. It was unclear to me how much of it he actually understood and assimilated until one day when I was driving with him to the airport. We had to drive past the exit to Southcenter Mall, which is one of his favorite places to go on outings. He likes to walk through all of the large department stores and ride the escalators and elevators. As we drove by he said, "Man take Southcenter Mall away in a truck?" This was his way of asking if Southcenter Mall was still there. I was puzzled by the question, as I could not imagine that an entire large mall had been closed. So I asked him why he was worried about it and he said, "News says shooting in Southcenter Mall; it is closed." I had been in Florida for the past month, so had not kept up with the news in Seattle. The next opportunity I had to talk to a local friend, I "fact-checked" Steven's information, and sure enough there had been a shooting in Southcenter Mall while we had been gone.

As our children become adults we don't always consciously think about it, but as parents we do have goals for them, the most important one being that they grow up to become happy, well adjusted adults who are able to make positive contributions to society which in turn helps them to be happy and fulfilled. As they get older we become more focused on the skills they will need to be able to function as mature adults. So as I watched Mark, Steven , and Geoff growing up, I began to realize that my goals for Steven were really the same as my goals were for Mark and Geoff. The only difference was that Steven had more challenges to overcome in order to acquire the necessary skills that he needed.

All of us need to feel that we are valued for what we can contribute; we need to feel that what we do in life is meaningful in order to feel fulfilled and content. These needs are no different for Steven than they are for any of us. And so, as Steven moved into the high school years, the focus in school changed from being academic, i.e. learning to read and do math, to learning job skills. The staff found job training opportunities outside of the classroom, and the students spent more and more time in the community at volunteer job locations learning specific skills that might lead to real jobs for them in the future.

This practical approach to learning was truly a "win win" situation for both the students and the community. By providing exposure to the students with special needs, the community learned that they are real, genuine, lovable young people, and not just faceless "scary labels".

We have been so fortunate to have lived in a smaller community where people feel more connected and more responsible for their neighbors; and to this day we are constantly amazed at how many people know and like Steven.  It seems that everywhere we go, someone comes up to us and introduces themselves as having known Steven in the past or present; these are people that we don't know and they always tell us how wonderful Steven is!!

Our school district had established a policy of "graduating" the Special Ed students from high school when they reached age 21. It so happened that I was the president of the School Board at the time of graduation for Steven so I had the honor of presenting him with his high school diploma.  After graduation, Steven moved into a new phase of his life with a whole new set of challenges.

# Students at NK high school are 'special'—

By RICK STEDMAN

It's the toughest job you'll ever love. That slogan is usually reserved for United States Peace Corps Volunteers. But at North Kitsap High School, Special Education instructor Jean Stephenson can surely boast that same phrase. Her reminder, which hangs on her office wall, is of a different variety. It says: Lord, grant me that I always desire more than I can accomplish. —Michelangelo

With March designated as National Mental Health Month, focus was given to the high school's Learning Center 3 program that governs those with learning disabilities.

"Our main emphasis is on the vocational skills, independent living skills, and social skills these students need in order to function in society," explained Stephenson.

At NKHS, 10 students are in the Special Education Program. All are 15-20 years old and have some form of mental or physical handicap.

So what does a handicap student do in a Special Ed class? "We have lots of vocational classes," said Stephenson. In addition to job skill training and social behavior classes, students may also take such things as film study, photography, music, and art. "We have one boy, Steve Rasmussen, who will be a great word processor," promised Stephenson.

Basically, Special Education students function in much the manner as other high school students. They ride school buses and eat in the cafeteria. However, their study skills center mostly on the vocational area, explained Stephenson, adding, "These kids are normal tenagers with a few problems."

Stephenson commended other high school students who reach out to those in Special Education. "It's really something the way they show their warmth, caring, and intelligence with these kids," she said.

## Acquiring skills

To acquire the much-needed social and work skills, students go out into the business community and work several hours a week. Stephenson and her aides arrange for the students to work at a variety of locations throughout North Kitsap and Bainbridge Island.

Some of those employers include the Marine Science Center, Market Place, Albertson's, IGA, St. Olaf's Catholic Church, Martha and Mary Nursing Home, Bloedel Timberlands Development Inc., Hostmark Apartments, and the Trident Refit Facility at Bangor.

"We have students working as janitors, paper shredders, gardeners, and some helping out with senior citizens," said Stephenson.

Twenty-year-old Derrick Van Gorder works at Bloedel Inc. on Bainbridge Island. "I work on trails, pick up sticks, and make the yard look pretty," he proudly said. Derrick sometimes works at Martha and Mary Nursing Home in Poulsbo.

Said Stephenson, "It's really neat to see these kids helping out our senior citizens at the nursing home." In addition to janitorial duties, the students help with feeding of the residents of Martha and Mary.

Another student, 17-year-old John Wasson, works as a janitor at St. Olaf's, while Daisy Williams, 16, works as a paper shredder at Martha and Mary. Daisy also works on occasion at Market Foods.

"What we're trying to do," said Stephenson, "is prepare these kids to work in society. For some, it will be a little harder, but they will be employable."

Stephenson, who's been involved with the Special Education Program for a year and a half at the high school, and five years overall, strongly feels that there's a need for more jobs in the community.

"They can do bus boy work and some, like Steve Rasmussen, will be excellent word processors," feels Stephenson. "I don't want to think in a limited fashion because there aren't many jobs that these kids can't do," she added.

The unemployment rate in the United States for the severely handicapped is about 60 percent, she said.

"It's to everyone's benefit that we try to employ as many special needs students as possible," said Stephenson.

Steve Rasmussen works on a computer when not serving as a janitor.    (photo by Rick Stedman)

*Newspaper clipping from Kitsap County Herald - March 30, 1988.*

and then!I get do holl lash the fun!things for yours birthday and how about eat
lunch out at silverdale bowlies alleys for rides elevators at four times at
silverdale bowlies alleys and silverdale computers stores for rides elevators
at two times at silverdale computers stores on!saturedar for yours birthday and
how about see the pond waters parks on!sunday for yours birthday o.k.!and how
about eat lunch out at kentuckey fried chickens at tacomas picnack parks on
sunday for yours birthday .o.k.!and how about tacomas zoos on!sunday for yours
birthday o.k.!and how about tacomas malls for rides elevators at six times at
tacomas malls on!sunday for yours birthday o.k.!and how about go the bon
marches for rides elevators at one times at the bon!marches on!sunday for yours
birthday o.k.!for tacomas malls for rides elevators at four times at tacomas
malls on!sunday for yours birthday o.k.!and how about go nordstrom for rides
elevators at two times at nordstrom on!sunday for yours birthday o.k.!and how
about go toys stores at tacomas malls on!sunday for yours birthday o.k.!and how
about go J.C.!Penneys for rides elevators at two times at J.C.!Penneys on
sunday for yours birthday o.k.!and how about go the bon!marches for rides
elevators at one times at the bon!marches on!sunday for yours birthday o.k.!for
yeady to go for go homes and how about take the red porsches cars for yours
birthday o.k.!and then!steven!mark geoffery mome and dade for well alls go to
doing something fun!on!sunday for yours birthday o.k.!and then!five peoples go
to doing something fun!on!sunday for yours birthday o.k.!and then!holl family
-n to doing something fun!on!sunday for yours birthday o.k.

*Early example of keyboarding - approximately 1991.*

102

*Steven at home in Washington - middle school age.*

*Steven keyboarding in high school.*

*Senior portraits.*

*Graduation.*

# PART III

## THE ADULT YEARS

# ABSTRACT CONCEPTS

### *UNDERSTANDING DEATH*

When Steven was 42, I found myself once more in a hospital room with him lying in the bed, and not knowing if he was going to live or die. Once more I was numb with fear; I was unable to think clearly or even to cry. I kept asking myself over and over again how did we get here? It was a huge step backward in time. Steven's life had been going so well; he had a good place to live after two years of tumultuous moving. At the time, he had a wonderful job that he loved, and where he was understood and supported by both management and his co-workers. Over the past year he had had to have all of his teeth removed and replaced with dentures, but he had adjusted well to this and seemed to be in good health.

When I started writing Steven's story, his life seemed to have stabilized, and I had planned to end the story on a happy note. But life doesn't always go according to plan and I was suddenly confronted with the harsh reality that there was a good possibility that I would outlive my child; something that no parent ever wants to have to contemplate.

Several days prior I received a call from the caregiver at Steven's group home informing me that Steven had not gone to work that day because he was sick with an upset stomach. We all agreed that it was best for him to stay home until he was well again. Then several hours later I received another call, this time again from the caregiver who had accompanied him to the emergency room of the local hospital. She said that he had ongoing diarrhea and vomiting, and that they were trying to get things stabilized but it looked like they would have to admit him rather than simply treat him and send him home.

Phil and I left immediately for the emergency room, which was a 45 minute drive away. When we arrived we were informed that an ambulance was on the way to transfer Steven to the main hospital in Bremerton where there was an ICU that would be better able to care for him; he needed more care than they were able to provide. They also explained to us that Steven was extremely dehydrated and that his blood pressure and heart rate were dangerously low. We followed the ambulance to the hospital and waited while he was admitted to the ICU. Several specialists were called in to examine him, one being a kidney specialist. He explained to us that the severe dehydration from the diarrhea and vomiting had caused Steven's kidneys to fail and that his blood pressure and heart rate were dangerously low. He did not mince words, telling us that Steven's condition was critical and he wasn't sure about the prognosis. We stayed until Steven went to sleep and there was nothing more we could do at the moment. We were physically and emotionally exhausted, so we went home to get some sleep.

The next week was a blur, with Phil and I taking turns staying at the hospital waiting for some news of improvement but receiving none. About the third day in, Phil talked with the kidney doctor, who was not at all encouraging, leaving us with the impression that we might need to make a decision about "pulling the plug" and letting Steven go in peace. The other possibility was that he might recover for awhile, but would spend the rest of his life on a dialysis machine. We were devastated; it all seemed like a nightmare. He was still in the ICU and the doctors were struggling to find the underlying cause of his intestinal problems. They were running almost continuous tests for infection identification and to check on kidney function. By the fourth day his kidneys were finally showing some improvement and it was decided to move him from the ICU to the regular ward.

Over the next few days he started to show a slow and steady improvement, but they still needed to find the cause of the infection, which had not gone away. He had been on IV fluids for days , but finally the doctors were able to start him on liquids, followed by soft foods. He tolerated all of these well, but the lab work and tests continued. They thought he was getting pneumonia and did a chest X-ray. He had an extended abdomen so an MRI was done, and the blood draws continued looking for a cause of the infection, which was persistent and which was being treated with high-powered drugs in hopes that they would knock it out.

The bright spot came from the visits by the kidney specialist; he said that Steven's kidneys were doing an amazing job of recovering and he was hopeful that he might make a complete recovery with no need for dialysis. This was a 100 degree turnaround from the previous prognosis so we were counting our blessings at this point. Finally the infection seemed to have abated and they decided that Steven could be discharged and go home. Phil and I celebrated that night at dinner, happily looking forward to having Steven back and on the road to a full recovery.

Our hopes were dashed the next morning by a phone call from the doctor at the hospital informing us that Steven had taken a turn for the worse overnight, and that they would be unable to let him go home. They were unclear as to what was going on, but he had spiked a very high fever and still had a serious infection.

Through all of this Steven had been a "super trooper", cooperative and compliant with everything he was asked to do; all of the blood draws, all of the tests, peeing in the bottle in his bed so that it could be measured, eating food and drinking liquids that he had never tried before because he was told that it would help him get better. He knew that he was sick and he had an amazing will to survive and recover. He talked about getting better, going back to work, and going on his "big trip" to Disney World in February. Everyone in the hospital who took care of him fell in love with him because he was so sweet and cooperative, never complaining about anything.

But when I went in to see him that morning there was a change. He was lying in the bed very still and quiet, almost unresponsive. He said to me, "Steven not better, Steven going to Heaven to see Jesus." It took every ounce of strength within me to hold it together at that moment and later out of his presence I found myself sobbing uncontrollably. The comfort was that I knew he would go to Heaven if we lost him, but it broke my heart that he knew he was so close to death and there was nothing that any of us could do about it.

Twenty four hours later, the picture changed again. The infection was identified, a hospital-borne infection that Steven had apparently contracted in the ICU, and the antibiotic was effective. Several days later, Steven was happily at home again and on the road to a full recovery. We weren't totally out of the woods; there were still numerous follow up appointments with a number of specialists, but in the end he received a clean bill of health for everything, including the kidneys, which had returned to completely normal functioning.

Abstract concepts are something that autistic people find especially difficult, and Steven is no exception. At an earlier age he would not have understood the concept of death, but he had had several earlier experiences which he was able to relate to his own brush with death. When he was about 8 years old, and we had recently completed our move to Washington, purchased the six acres and completed building our home, we also constructed a barn. Being young and idealistic Phil and I had pictured ourselves as becoming partially self-sufficient on this acreage, buying some farm animals, having a large garden and raising at least some of our own food. So we proceeded to purchase two baby pigs and constructed a pig pen adjacent to the horse barn. We also had a horse, which we bought because I had one as a kid, and thought the boys might enjoy it too. One morning we became aware of a noisy commotion down by the barn, so we hurried down to check. When we got there we found a very upset horse chasing one baby pig, and the other baby pig lying prone on the ground. Closer examination confirmed what we had feared; both pigs had managed to escape their pen and had entered the horse barn. In the fray that followed one of the pigs had been kicked to death by the horse. Steven was with us, taking it all in intently, and saying that he wanted the pig to get up and walk. We explained to him that the pig could not get up and walk again; that the pig was dead and that we would need to bury it in the ground. He watched soberly as we took care of the problem, and we explained to him that although the pig would never get up and walk again, it was okay because the pig didn't hurt anymore. He talked about this for a long time afterwards, but apparently was able to assimilate it.

Sometime later, when Steven was yet a little older, he again came into contact with a death. Phil had an aunt and uncle living in Bremerton when we moved to Washington, and they became like second grandparents to our children. They were wonderful, even babysitting for us upon occasion, and the children were quite close to them. Then one day we learned that Aunt Katy was very ill with a brain tumor. When she was near death, we took the children to see her in the hospital and say good-bye to her. She died shortly thereafter, and this experience made a huge impression on Steven. He was worried about Aunt Katy being buried in the ground like the baby pig, so we explained to him that people were different, that they went to Heaven to be with Jesus. He wanted to know where Heaven was, so we told him simply that it was way up in the sky and that it was a happy place to be when we die. We also explained that Jesus would take care of Katy and that she wasn't sick anymore.

He seemed to understand and accept that explanation and was not upset about Katy's death after that. But it was only after he was facing death himself that I fully realized how well he understood what it meant, and his innocent and accepting faith is truly an inspiration to me.

## *UNDERSTANDING CAUSE AND EFFECT*

Another abstract concept that is difficult for autistic people to understand is that of cause and effect. An example of this occurred when Steven became concerned about seeing cars that were pulled off to the side of the road when we were out driving with him in the car. He correctly understood that cars should be driving down the road, and not pulled off to the side, so he was concerned about why this happened. He was afraid that it might also happen to our car when we were driving. We explained to him that maybe the car had engine trouble or maybe it had run out of gas.

When he was with us and we needed gas, we taught him how to pump the gas. This became an activity that he really enjoyed, and he always insisted on pumping the gas for us. Therefore, he now focused on the explanation that maybe the cars on the side of the road had run out of gas; and it was now clear to him that it took gas to make the car run. After this he carefully watched the gas gauge on our car, and became quite concerned if it appeared that the gauge was low. He also insisted that we turn off the engine if we stopped the car for any reason other than a stoplight, telling us that he didn't want to "waste gas."

A new breakthrough in understanding the concept of cause and effect occurred a number of years later when we were sitting in an airplane at the gate waiting for the plane to leave the gate for take-off. Steven was sitting in the window seat watching the activity outside of the plane. The gas truck was beside the plane and the workers were pumping the gas into the plane's fuselage. After watching this activity for a few minutes, Steven turned to me with a worried look on his face and said, "Airplane needs gas to go; airplane not run out of gas?", his way of asking whether or not the airplane could run out of gas just like the cars. Of course I reassured him that the airplane would have plenty of gas, that the plane would not run out of gas and drop out of the sky, as he was imagining. It was interesting though, how many years it took, and how Steven needed very concrete examples in order to understand that concept, but he was able to eventually make the connection.

# A PLACE TO LIVE

A safe and comfortable place to live is something that most Americans take for granted. It is expected that our parents will provide us with that first safe haven; a home where we can grow, develop and thrive as we strive to reach adulthood. Eventually the day arrives when we are expected to "leave the nest", strike out on our own and establish a new home, a new safe haven for ourselves and the families we will create as the next generation. As with everything in life, there are variations as to how and when this occurs for each child, but ultimately the reality is that parents pass away and children need to be able to survive independently without the physical presence and support of their parents.

In most families, this rite of passage occurs naturally and gradually over time. But for families with a "special needs" child, this process takes on a whole new meaning. Often the parents of these children are so overwhelmed in the early years with simply caring for the child and managing their special problems, that planning for the future is pushed into the background to be faced at a later date. But as the child becomes a teenager, suddenly this "later date" is now, and it becomes apparent that planning needs to be done for this child's future.

Parents are often torn between keeping the child at home and continuing to care for him/her for as long as they are physically able to do so, or finding some kind of outside placement. Making a decision for outside placement can trigger feelings of guilt about not loving your child enough to care for him/her at home forever. There is also concern about placing the burden of care on the child's siblings, because most parents want their other children to be able to live a normal life, being able to get married and have children of their own without having to worry about the care of their disabled sibling, at least on a daily basis. And like most other parents of a special needs child, Phil and I struggled with our mixed feelings and emotions in dealing with this issue.

We had both grown up hearing about the dismal and dreaded

"institutions" where the mentally disabled and ill were destined to live out their lives, and in our minds, this was the last place we would ever consider allowing our child to be placed. When Steven was first diagnosed with autism at the UCLA Neuropsychiatric Institute, we were told that unless he learned to talk before he was four years old, he was probably destined to live a life in an institution, and they were not holding out very much hope that he would ever learn to talk. We were devastated, but I vowed at that moment that this would never happen to my child! However, when he became a teenager we also realized that it would not be healthy for him or for us to have him stay forever in our home.

Over the years Steven had made great strides; not only did he learn to talk before he was four years old, but he learned to read, write, and do simple arithmetic. His behavior was under control and he learned how to be socially appropriate most of the time. What we realized was that Steven had benefited greatly from the many dedicated teachers and other professionals who had contributed to his growth and development over the years, and that we had been essentially successful in achieving "normalization" for him in large areas of his life. At this point our goal was to continue that process, and most normal young adults did not stay at home forever, they moved out of the family home and started new lives in homes of their own. We decided that it would be important for Steven to make this same transition, and it needed to happen while we were still alive to facilitate it for him. We realized that if Steven stayed at home with us until we were gone, that it would be a huge shock for him if we died and it became necessary to move him into a different situation.

In both California and Washington, as soon as a child is identified as having a disability, he is certified as eligible for services from the state agency and is assigned a caseworker. The state agency in Washington is the Department of Social and Health Services (DSHS). It was our plan that when Steven was finished with school, we would work with his caseworker from DSHS to find an appropriate place for him to live.

When Steven was still in his last year of high school, just by coincidence, Phil was on a special committee at our local church that was involved in providing food for the needy. The subject of the Pastor moving out of the parsonage and the church needing to find a new use for the now vacant parsonage came up at one of the meetings. That got Phil's attention and he immediately seized upon the opportunity to explore the possibility of using the parsonage for a new Group Home in our small community where none currently existed, citing the need for one due to the fact that a number of young people would soon be graduating from the current high school Special Ed class.

The same parents who had been instrumental in working with us to start the summer program for Special Ed were now interested in finding appropriate places for our young people to live following graduation from high school. Phil and I along with Jean and Jack W., arranged a meeting with our caseworker from DSHS, Peter D. to discuss the possibility of opening a new licensed Group Home at the parsonage location. Two key issues would be funding and staffing, both of which would require Peter's guidance and assistance.

Peter was very supportive of our idea and encouraged us to pursue it, so we had a follow up meeting with the church and found them also to be very encouraging. Ultimately, we were able to succeed in our efforts, and opened a lovely new group home for our young adults who needed a warm and caring place to live. The parsonage was in a small, nice older neighborhood within walking distance of the downtown Poulsbo area. The home was on two levels and had five bedrooms, four bathrooms, and several large recreational/living areas. We were able to staff it with a family that consisted of a working Dad, a stay at home Mom and a four-year-old little boy whom everyone loved. We were able to accommodate six residents but we opened with only two, John W. and Steven.

After Jean W. and I worked together with the administrators in our school district to initiate a summer program for Special

Education students, we both later participated in other volunteer efforts to help people with disabilities in our community. One was working with a group that was trying to establish transportation services for people with special needs who were unable to ride the regular bus. At the time that we were opening the new group home, both Jean and I were on our local school board, an elected volunteer position with four-year terms. This responsibility consumed hours of our time, but we believed in the goal of providing the best possible education for all of the students in our community and both of us felt it was well worth the time and effort. So by the time we were ready to open the group home, we had already spent many hours working together on similar projects. We also had the backing of two very supportive spouses who participated in this effort. In addition, we were now familiar with the support agencies in our community and had credibility and contacts within those agencies.

Our two sons had different medical conditions, but we had learned that the special needs of those with disabilities were often very similar. John's diagnosis was Down's Syndrome and Steven's was Autism. Next we received a referral through our caseworker at DSHS for another resident, Tony, who was a young man in a wheelchair with no cognitive deficits but who had a severe kidney disorder and required frequent dialysis and numerous trips to the Kidney Center. Tony was similar in age to Steven and John, he got along well with them and fit right into the family life of our newly created group home.

The caregivers, Pat and "Big John", did a wonderful job of taking care of "our guys", and when they needed an occasional break or had a personal emergency either Jean or I or our spouses would step in and cover in their absence. The home ran smoothly for several years with our three original residents, and from time to time it also provided respite care for one or more residents on a temporary basis. But eventually, "Big John" received an offer of employment for a better job located out of state, so Pat and John moved away.

When this happened, we turned to Peter D., our caseworker at DSHS for help in locating new caregivers. We were unable to find anyone who wanted to live in the home full time as Pat and John had done, so we ended up staffing it with part time people who had other jobs with other agencies, but were willing to fill in extra hours staffing our home. Some of our part time helpers were very good, but others not so much, so we spent more time than any of us wanted to just managing problems at the home.

A large part of the problem was that we were unable to offer very much money for staff members, as we were dependent on state formulas for funding, and it just wasn't enough to attract or keep good people. We realized how fortunate we had been in having Pat and John who were willing to use the free rent as part of their compensation. Combined with the fact that John had an outside job, what we were able to offer as a salary had been sufficient.

After about a year of operating on a shoestring we had an event that was the final blow to us being able to continue our effort. Sadly, Tony went to the hospital with an emergency and did not survive. Besides being saddened by his loss, we realized that we could no longer continue as we had. Additionally, the circumstances had changed for the church. They had a new Pastor, and he expressed a desire to live in the parsonage. So at the end of our lease we disbanded the home and John moved to a ranch in eastern Washington, while Phil and I found a group home for Steven that was located closer to us in our community.

We were about to embark on an entirely new and foreign experience, navigating the world of licensed group homes for the placement of a loved family member. Heretofore, we had had almost total control over Steven's environment and the care he received. First he was at home with us for 19 years, then he was in a group home that we had control over and where we were constantly monitoring the level of care. Now, in someone else's group home, we found that we had very little knowledge or control over what happened to him in that home.

One of the things we have always done is to make sure that Steven spends at least two to six days a month with us at our home, usually on his days off from work. Since his verbal communication is limited, we did not always get a good description of his life in the group home, but instead had to rely on the gauge of whether or not he was happy about being returned to the home after his visit with us. It didn't take very long for us to realize that Steven really was not very happy in this next group home, so we started asking questions and talking to Peter D., our caseworker, about his impression of the home. Peter then also started asking some questions, and what we learned was that the home was basically unsupervised most of the time. There were four to five young adults of both sexes residing in the home at any given time, and during the day they were left on their own for many hours at a time. Since Steven does not have the skills required for a great deal of social interaction, this meant that most of the time when he was not at work or visiting with us, he was lying in his bed by himself doing nothing. Together, Peter, Phil and I determined that Steven needed to be moved and a new placement was located.

After one or two failed placements similar to the first failure, we finally found a home for Steven that was compatible with his needs. Instead of a group home, he was placed into a non-licensed but approved individual family home. The family consisted of a stay at home mom, a father who was in the home during part of the day, but was also working outside of the home in other placement settings for disabled adults, and eight year old twin boys who were their children. Steven had his own bedroom in the basement, and the twins liked Steven, and engaged him in many of their activities.

During this time Steven had some behavioral issues, as he was experiencing a delayed adolescence in his early twenties. He would become frustrated, often with no apparent provocation, and would jump up and down, bite his hands, and make an unpleasant high pitched shrieking noise. Mike and Emma were able to take this in stride; we had discussions with them about strategies for managing the behavior, and we worked with the caseworker to procure an extensive psychiatric evaluation for Steven with the end result that he was placed on some much needed medication that significantly impacted his quality of life and his ability to cope with his environment.

At this juncture in Steven's story, I would like to interject a discussion regarding the use of medications for behavior control. For many years I had adamantly rejected any use of medication for behavior. In my opinion this would be simply masking the problem instead of dealing with it, and producing a zombie-like personality instead of the real person who was my child. I now deeply regret having stuck to my guns on that decision for as long as I did, and I have no one except myself to blame for this. As we begin to understand more about autism and its causes, we realize more and more that it is a disorder with biological and sometimes genetic roots and that brain chemistry plays a very large role in behaviors, not only in this disorder, but many others as well. Therefore, medications that can alter brain chemistry without having too many side effects can significantly increase the quality of life for a person who suffers from behavioral disorders.

In the alternative, a person who is unable to function at an acceptable level in society will eventually be removed from that society and placed into an institution where the unacceptable behavior can be managed. I did not want that outcome for Steven and had I understood years earlier what a difference the medication would make for him, I most certainly would have made a different decision when he was much younger. So today when I am asked by parents of younger autistic children for my opinion about the use of medications, my unequivocal answer is that it most certainly should be seriously considered as an option. They should discuss it with their child's physician, and use it if recommended by that physician.

Returning to our journey through the world of "out of home" placements; once Phil and I had made the decision to go forward with that option we did not want to reverse direction. Since we had almost total control over the first placement, our initial reaction was that it had a positive result for both Steven and us. Then we had the negative experience with several more placements that did not work out very well, but Steven had a very good experience in the family home with Mike and Emma. This situation lasted for 10 years until the twins graduated from high school, then things changed dramatically. They moved out of their home; one to go to college and the other to live in his own apartment. Soon we noticed that Mike was never in the home when we came to take Steven for his visits with us. We also noticed a change in Emma; she was distant and withdrawn, and once more Steven was left basically alone with nothing to do except lie in bed most of the time. Mike was the licensed caregiver for Steven, but he was never there. When the caseworker came for the annual recertification, Emma was the only one present besides me, and she informed the caseworker that Mike was no longer available. The caseworker informed Emma that the recertification could not be done without Mike, that Mike had to be present in the home as a primary caregiver, and that no further payments could be made by DSHS for Steven's care in this home.

The caseworker and I had previously discussed the deficiencies of this placement for Steven and had agreed that we needed to move him. The difficulty arose in finding a home for him that had an opening. At this point, homes with openings were few and far between, but legally Steven had to be moved within 24 hours of the casework determination that Mike was no longer present in the home. We were presented with the option of taking him home with us and being paid for his care, which I immediately and adamantly rejected. I explained to the caseworker that this would be a giant step backward in our life plan for Steven; that he had adjusted to moving out of the family home as would be expected of any normal adult, and that it would be very deleterious for him to be bouncing back and forth between our home and other placements, expecting him to readjust over and over again. She understood and was able to find another home that was newly licensed.

Steven's home with Emma had become extremely messy and even downright dirty by the time he moved, so the new home was like a breath of fresh air. It was a brand new mobile home located on a large lot with open space and woods around it. The family operating the home was a husband/wife team. The husband was a truck driver, so was gone a quite a bit, but the wife was there all of the time. She was assisted by an adult married son who lived on an adjacent property with his family; while the husband and wife lived in another nearby house. So the home was a "stand alone" home for the residents, but was staffed by various members of the family.

Steven was the second young adult to be placed in this home; the first was another young man, about Steven's age, who was also diagnosed with autism. This young man was "high functioning" with more social skills than Steven, but he liked Steven and they got along very well together. The family was busy and active and included the two residents in their activities, so Steven had things to do and was not just sitting around bored when he was not at work.

Once more we were happy and hopeful about Steven's living situation. It appeared that the family was committed to the long term, as they had invested a lot of money and time into the physical facility as well as the staffing and management requirements. After Steven moved in, another young man joined them, and then a series of individuals followed who were not compatible with the home and who were quickly moved out. The home was licensed for six beds, and really needed to occupy at least four to five of them to remain economically viable. Unfortunately, due to economic pressure to fill the vacancies, and the relative inexperience of this family in operating a group home for disabled people, the severely physically disabled clients they accepted exhausted their time resources.

They also accepted both sexes, including at least one person who was mentally disturbed. That placement turned out to be a disaster for the family and to everyone living in the home. She was in her late teens, attractive and flirtatious. When the owner's married son, who was in his 30's and had a child of his own, was on duty, this young lady made the claim that he had made inappropriate advances to her. As soon as DSHS received word of this accusation and without any investigation, the home was immediately closed down and everyone was moved out. The caseworker barely had time to inform us that they were moving Steven within hours and would let us know where he was as soon as they could.

We don't know if the son of the caregiver was guilty or not, but to us closing the home seemed like a drastic measure. To our way of thinking, it would have been more reasonable to simply bar him from being in the home until a complete investigation could take place instead of displacing four or five other residents who had no place to go. So the living situation for which we had held such high hopes for stability and permanency evaporated in less than six months. Fortunately, temporary homes were found for all of the residents; however, Steven had bonded with the caregiver and some of her family members, so he was sad and didn't understand why he had to be moved.

His "temporary" placement was in a licensed group home that was centrally located and had five adult male residents. The caregiver/owner, Nancy, was close to my age, retired and in the home 24/7. The residents of the home had all been there for at least six to ten years, so it was a stable situation for all of them. After a short time, it was apparent that Steven was happy in this situation. Nancy invited him to stay, and the caseworker and Phil and I agreed that it would be a good home for Steven. He remained in this home for five years, and we had hoped for many more, but Nancy developed some serious health problems. She started having breathing difficulties and was on oxygen. Her adult son, James, lived with her, and she started training him to take over many of the care-taking duties. Pretty soon James was doing most of the caregiving and Nancy was in and out of the hospital.

Shortly thereafter we received a message from our caseworker, Vikka, that Nancy had passed away, and that Steven would need to be moved in the next 24 hours, as there was no longer a licensed caregiver in the home. James was trying to complete the requirements for being licensed and we were willing to leave Steven in place until that happened, but the law was clear, there were no exceptions, the home would be closed immediately. We were once more struggling to find a good place for Steven to live, and the timing of this closure could not have been worse.

Over the past five years or so, Phil and I had achieved a degree of financial freedom that allowed us to purchase a second home in a warm climate, so we had become "snowbirds", leaving in late October to drive to southern Florida, where we own a condominium on the beach. This particular year we had made arrangements to meet friends on November 1st, meaning that we had to keep a semblance of a schedule for the drive down. We also wanted to visit some family members along the way, so we had specific dates for each place we were stopping, and I had made reservations for almost every night along our route. Some of these reservations could have been cancelled but most were non-refundable, and to change our plans for any part of the trip had implications for the entire trip and would have cost us several thousand dollars.

It was exactly a day and a half before we were scheduled to leave when we got the phone call from the caseworker about Nancy and the home having to close. And for the first time I felt truly angry at the system that was so inflexible and uncaring about how many lives it disrupted or destroyed. At this point Steven had a very good job that required him to be where public transportation was available, and this job was truly the most important thing in his life. We felt that it was critical for him to keep the job and that a home must be found in a location that allowed him to do so. Yet we were being told that there were no openings any place in our county and that the only option DSHS could see was to move Steven out of county to adjacent Pierce county which was many miles south of our home, our community, his job and in a large city that we felt was unsafe, Tacoma.

I was ready to take legal action if necessary, but in the interim we would have to cancel our trip, forfeit the deposits, bring Steven home and transport him to work ourselves, which was a 1 ½ hour round trip two times a day in order for him to keep his job. We were very unhappy about the situation and I didn't mince words in letting the caseworker know how we felt. To her credit, once she understood the urgency of the situation for us, she found a place where we were able to take Steven that very evening. We rushed around, picking him up from the old home that was now closed, explaining to him why he was being moved and talking to him about the new house, trying to reassure him that everything was going to be okay. We determined that all of the transportation arrangements had been made so that he would not lose his job, and after arriving at the new home we found his new bedroom and helped to get him settled in as best as possible. The next day Phil and I left on schedule for our 4,000 mile driving trip across the country to Florida.

Two days later as we were driving from California to Arizona I received an emergency phone call from Steven's caseworker, Vikka. We all knew that this had been a temporary solution, but even so, it had gotten off to a bad start. Vikka informed me that the new caregiver, Valerie, was unwilling to keep Steven for any longer than was absolutely necessary because Valerie felt that he was too much of a liability in her home.

I was astounded! He had been in his previous home for five years until it was forced to close due to the death of the caregiver; he had been in the home before that until it was forced to close because of allegations against a caregiver that had nothing to do with Steven, and he was in his home before that for 10 years until it was closed because the licensed caregiver had moved out due to divorce. When I asked the reason why it was so imperative to immediately move him again, I was informed that Valerie had read all of the prior assessments apparently dating back for years, and decided that Steven was really a big problem to take care of and she did not want the responsibility.

Once a person enters the DSHS system, they need to be re-certified once a year, both as to their eligibility for services and for the appropriateness of the services they are receiving. This entails an interview with the client receiving the services, the legal guardian, and the caregiver where the client resides. The amount of funding received by the caregiver from the state (DSHS) depends on the level of services being provided. The more disabled the client, the greater the need for more intense services, and the greater the reimbursement or funding to the caregiver from the state.

Having been a provider ourselves when we ran our group home, I realized how meager the funding is compared to the real needs of our developmentally disabled family members, so in the past when I realized that a caregiver needed to understate Steven's actual abilities and overstate his needs in order to receive adequate funding to meet his actual needs, I did not correct the record or object to the assessment. Instead, I dutifully went along with whatever the caseworker and caregiver decided, and signed the document without comment. I did not realize that whatever went into that assessment would follow Steven for the rest of his life.

For example, when Steven was a teenager and before he was on regular medication, some of his behaviors were more difficult to manage. He knew that the street could be dangerous, and one of his self-destructive behaviors was to run out into the street when he was upset. This behavior was of course very upsetting to the adults who were in charge of his care. However, once he was on the medication the behavior stopped, but it continued to be listed as a problem in the record every year from then on.

There were other mistakes in the record that had serious consequences for Steven each time that he had to be moved. As a result of his multiple bowel surgeries as an infant, he was left with a bowel leakage problem for the rest of his life. While it is not generally a problem, it does present management difficulties when his stomach is upset and he has diarrhea. He has always tried to clean himself up after using the bathroom, but sometimes this is a messy proposition and has less than wonderful results. So every caregiver has noted this as a special need in his annual assessment, which is an accurate statement of need. However, at some point along the line, someone stated that Steven was deliberately smearing feces in the bathroom, a totally false and unfair statement about his behavior. Yet once this was in the record it continued to follow him and was given credence by new caregivers until I found out about it and insisted on clarification.

One last incident that happened recently and was extremely troubling to us occurred when one of the caregivers allowed the residents to sort their own laundry from mixed loads with the clothing items of four or five other residents. Steven is perfectly capable of doing his own laundry, sorting it out, folding it and putting it away as long as it is not mixed with the items belonging to other people. He pays no attention whatsoever to his clothing and would not have any idea what belongs to him and what doesn't when it is all mixed together. He tries very hard to be cooperative and to please others, so when asked to sort and fold the laundry he would make a good attempt to comply, but would be confused about which things belonged to whom. So one of the caregivers in one of the less desirable recent placements decided that Steven was "stealing" other "people's" clothing.

Steven does not know how to defend himself, and indeed would not even know what it means to steal something, although if he knows an item belongs to someone else he will not take it, EVER. So I was incensed when I heard this accusation. Again, it was impossible to correct the record once the accusation had been made without requesting a huge formal hearing and probably making the situation for Steven even worse, so it was not worth the effort, time and emotional energy.

When Vikka informed us about the new situation with Steven, I asked her if he had actually done anything to prompt this removal request from Valerie, and the answer was no. At this point I was envisioning that we would have to turn around and drive back to Washington, but she said that Valerie would not be able to simply put Steven out if there was no place for him to go. We ended the conversation with Vikka telling us that she would try to find a new placement as soon as possible, and that she would do the physical moving when that happened.

Since we are Steven's legal guardians, except in emergencies, caseworkers cannot just make a decision to move him without our authorization. This is why it is so important for parents or a responsible relative to obtain legal guardianship as soon as the disabled person reaches the age of 18 years old. Years ago, when Phil and I took this step, I was so trusting of the various governmental agencies involved that I hadn't been sure that it was really necessary. I assumed that these agencies would always make decisions that would be in Steven's best interest, but over the years I learned over and over again that a bureaucracy is faceless, mindless and heartless; that rules reign supreme, even those that are conflicting, and bureaucrats, even well meaning ones, are bound to abide by the rules of the system as it is being interpreted at the time, regardless of whether or not the decisions make sense, and never mind whether or not they are in the best interest of the disabled person.

In less than two months, Vikka found another group home that had an opening, and moved him once more. When we returned to Washington for the Christmas holidays we went to visit the new group home and meet the caregivers. We received a pretty chilly reception and were at first puzzled by this, as we had not had any negative reports about Steven from Vikka in this new home; but it did not take very long for the reason to become apparent. The home was located in the far south end of the county and was miles away from Steven's job. His special Access bus stopped short of the group home by about five miles, requiring a 20 minute roundtrip drive to be made by someone in order to get him all of the way home. Since we had been so insistent that his placement in any group home had to allow him access to his job, my assumption is that the caseworker told the staff that it would be their responsibility to get him back and forth from the last bus stop where he was dropped off. I also believe that they felt pressured to take Steven in order to fill all of their beds and they were led to believe that if they didn't give him at least a trial, there would be no more referrals to their group home. At any rate, we began to hear the complaints immediately regarding the inconvenience of having to transport him back and forth to the bus stop. We were sympathetic to their complaint and offered to pay extra for this service, but they turned down the offer. We also noted during our visits to the home that the other residents were all fairly high functioning; they interacted with each other socially and required very little outside assistance in being able to care for themselves. Therefore, very little was required of the caregivers, and in turn they did very little. The other residents were avid computer game players, and that's about all we ever saw them doing anytime we were there.

Since Steven does not initiate social interaction or activity, he required more assistance from the caregivers when he was not at work. He knows how to cook simple meals but needs assistance in shopping and organizing the cooking activity. He wears dentures, and needs assistance in the care of the dentures. He has trouble managing personal hygiene in the bathroom with his bowel problem, and although he has always been able to dress himself, he requires help in choosing appropriate and clean clothing. He also was unable to pick his clothing out of the community laundry basket, fold it and put it away because he didn't know which clothes were his. He loves to do yard work outside, but we were told that they would not allow him to be outside by himself for fear that he might wander away or behave inappropriately in front of neighborhood children in spite of the fact that there was no evidence that he would do either.

What we eventually learned was that James, the adult son of Nancy who was trying to obtain a license for managing that home before Nancy passed away, had sabotaged Steven's placement in Valerie's home by telling Valerie that Steven was a "runner", which was patently untrue. Then when James was unable to obtain the license to reopen Nancy's home, he became an employee of the new home where Steven was currently residing. All of the complaints about the difficulty in caring for Steven were coming from James, and we have never been able to figure out why. Steven lived in Nancy's house for five years, and she loved him. She always had nothing but praise for him, he liked her and was happy in her home. We had always been nice to James and were very sad and sympathetic to him when his mother died, so his negative attitude about Steven made no sense to us.

By the time Phil and I returned to Washington in the spring it was apparent that this new placement was not going to work. The owner made a formal request for Steven's removal and we also were no longer willing to have him in that situation. The owner did not live in the home, but rather had periodic meetings with his employees, and even though at least two of the employees were clearly lying about Steven, the owner took the position that he had to rely on their reports. Vikka made several visits, she and I had a joint meeting with the owner, and she and I came to the same conclusion about the situation; that the employees wanted to fill the beds in this home with residents who required the least amount of care. Since there was a shortage of beds in the county, group home owners had choices about who they would accept, and obviously they wanted to have those folks who were the highest functioning and the least amount of work.

This is yet another example of how the bureaucracy fails those who are most in need in our communities. If the system worked efficiently and fairly every group home would have a mix of easy and more difficult residents and they would all receive payment in accordance to the level of services they were actually providing. No home would be allowed to accept only the "easy" clients while another was overburdened with all difficult clients, and there would be no need to exaggerate a client's needs in order to receive higher compensation. Instead, there would be fair compensation for everyone based on actual and real needs.

At this point Vikka was exploring every possible option for Steven and we were beginning to seriously doubt our decision of years ago to help Steven move out of our home and become as independent as possible. Still, we knew the clock was ticking and that eventually we would be too old to care for him. We also wanted to have services in place that would allow our other adult children, Steven's siblings, to be able to live their lives as normally as possible. We knew that they would need to eventually take over the guardianship duties, but we did not want them to have to take the responsibility for his physical everyday care 24/7.

Thankfully, at the end of May, Vikka called to say that there was an opening in a home located close to Steven's job, and within easy driving distance for us to visit him too. She said that the owners wanted to meet Steven before they made a decision and as required by law, they had received all of the records from DSHS, including those that contained inaccuracies about his behavior. So it was with more than a little anxiety and trepidation that we visited the home first by ourselves and then with Steven. However, our anxiety was unfounded; the home was the nicest group home I had ever seen. It was immaculate inside and out, and still warm and welcoming. The quality of the interior was outstanding; hardwood floors, granite counters, new stainless steel kitchen appliances, and comfortable new furniture. No one would ever guess that this was a group home for disabled adults, there was no hint of "institutionalism". Then we met the owners, a couple in their mid-fifties; the husband was retired military and his wife was from the Philippines. It appeared that the caregivers were all family and friends of the wife, and all were so open and nice to us. They were also conscientious and hardworking, and they exhibited a real understanding and caring attitude towards the residents in their care. It was such a breath of fresh air after all that we had been through with a search for a home for Steven in the past year.

We had an open and frank discussion with the owner and his wife about the negative reports regarding Steven's behavior in the recent home placements, and they were very open to reserving judgment until they had an opportunity to get to know Steven and see what kind of an adjustment he would make in their home. We immediately felt that Steven would do very well here, it was exactly the calm and caring environment that he needed in order to thrive. Our predictions were correct and Steven fulfilled the trial period without problems, fitting easily into the daily life of this wonderful group home.

The owners, James and his wife Ehrly, own two group homes serving a total of 11 or 12 residents at any given time. This is their retirement career and they are totally dedicated to doing a good job. A funny coincidence about this home is that after Steven moved in, we realized that one of the residents in the home was John W., Steven's classmate from years ago whose parents co-founded that first group home with Phil and myself. Over the years, we had lost track of John since he had moved out of the area, and his parents, Jean and Jack W., were about 10 to 15 years our senior, so we did not see them socially either once our group home was closed. In the interval, Jack had passed away, and we recently learned that Jean had also passed away, so now John's siblings were looking after him. John is probably the resident with the most intense needs in the home, as he is not verbal and spends much of his time rocking back and forth and making strange loud noises. Nevertheless, James and Ehrly are very patient with him and take loving care of him.

Steven has been in this home now for almost three years and we consider this to be the happy ending that we always wished to have in finding a home for him. Whenever we talk to James about Steven, he always tells us how he wishes all of his residents could be as easy as Steven, and that they are so happy to have him there. That is music to our ears, and we hope and pray that James and Ehrly will be around for a very long time.

I think we have reached a point in this country where there are many elderly or aging parents of adult disabled children who desperately need to know that their child will have stability when they are gone. All of us want our child to have a clean, healthy and caring living environment. We want to know that there are daily activities that are enjoyable and fulfilling for our adult child. This should include work activities and leisure activities that are appropriate for the individual's level of functioning. We don't want him to be warehoused in an institution, nor do we want him to be bounced around from place to place and job to job. Most of all, we do not feel it is appropriate or necessary for siblings to be totally responsible for the daily care of our adult disabled person or for having to take him into their own homes to live.

My ideal model would be a small community within the larger community where there would be a number of small cottages and a 24-hour caregiver in each one. Jobs would be found in the community where the employer was provided with extra incentives to employ those disabled persons who are able to work, and someone would be responsible for developing job sites where appropriate placements could be made. There would be organized leisure activities for each resident, including outings into the community. There would be transportation dedicated to meeting the needs of this community, and the placement of the individual in the community would be permanent.

We are aware that some parents and organizations are working on similar concepts, but we are not there yet. Until every developmentally disabled person, including those with autism, has the stability that would be provided by a model similar to this, we have unfinished business.

# THE JOB QUEST

One evening I was sitting in front of the television watching the news when the ad flashed on. Normally my mind clicks into neutral for the ads but this one caught my attention immediately. It showed a young person with Down's Syndrome sitting very still in the shadows of a darkened room. A quiet voice came on and asked, "What is the worst thing that can happen to this person?" Then in large letters across the bottom of the screen came the word: "NOTHING". This was followed by an announcement that the ad was sponsored by an organization that provided services for young people with developmental disabilities.

This is one of the most powerful and effective ads I have ever seen and it really hit home for us in our struggles to help Steven find and keep a job.

When Steven turned 21 years old in 1992 he was no longer eligible to remain in the public school system program. During the last several years that he had been in the high school Special Ed program, there had been an emphasis placed on preparing him for the workplace, so we were anxious to help him find a job as soon as possible after he left school. The parent group that Jean and Jack W. and Phil and I had founded while our students were still in school was named Parent Supported Employment in anticipation of the day we would need to help our students find jobs. In the meantime, the opportunity to open the group home presented itself and was also an urgent need in our community, so we concentrated our efforts on that. But now we were faced with the need for employment, and found that no employment services were available for young adults with developmental disabilities.

At this point it seemed to us that Steven's needs for job development and placement services were unique and different from the other students in his class who had a variety of different disabilities. Steven was the only student who was autistic and he had a different skill set and deficits than the students with Down's Syndrome or other types of mental retardation. Many years ago when he had been tested, he had a non verbal IQ that was within a normal range, and we had known for a very long time that he was quite capable of understanding most of what was said to him. His deficit was in being able to respond to questions and in initiating conversations and social interactions.

Phil and I proceeded to do a job search for Steven. He had done a job as a volunteer from the Special Ed classroom in a restaurant with duties as a bus boy, janitor, and dishwasher; so this was our first choice as the type of job that we sought for him. We were fortunate in finding a job opening at a very nice restaurant on nearby Bainbridge Island with similar duties. The job was well within Steven's capabilities but he needed training in order to understand exactly what was expected of him. He also needed to know the order in which he was to perform the various tasks, because one of the deficits of autism is an inability to be spontaneous. As long as the job had an orderly progression of duties he performed well. He could also change direction if specifically asked to do so; but he was incapable of anticipating a need to do something if it was not on the list.

Phil and I promised to do the "on the job" training with Steven for as long as necessary and we were also required to provide all of the transportation. This meant that Phil and I were essentially taking turns working for the restaurant for whatever hours were assigned to Steven. Fortunately, we were both self-employed at the time and therefore we could adjust our schedules in order to cover Steven's job.

This worked wonderfully well for the restaurant; they had an employee who was 100% reliable, never absent and always on time, who did a very good job because there were also two supervisors with college degrees on site making sure that things went well. Eventually, Phil and I determined it was time for us to begin to fade out. We gradually reduced our hours until Steven was there most of the time on his own. It was then that we began to receive complaints about Steven's performance. From the nature of the complaints we could tell that the problems were not really a result of his not being able to do the job, but rather that the restaurant staff felt insecure about being able to communicate with him and also that they expected more spontaneity from him than was possible; i.e. an expectation that he would notice the floor was dirty and sweep it without being asked or out of sequence from when it would be done on his list of duties. The end result was that Steven was dismissed, but the positive was that he now had some real job experience with which to go forward in looking for a new job.

Since Steven was receiving Social Security income, everything he earned had to be reported to Social Security and also to his caseworker at DSHS. It was when we were discussing the loss of the job with the caseworker that we first learned about a resource for Steven to help him with employment. It was unclear then and still is now as to whether or not this resource had been available from the day Steven left school, but we were grateful to learn about it and to know that we were not solely responsible for finding a job and doing the on-site job training.

The caseworker referred Steven to the state agency that was responsible for paying unemployment benefits and helping find employment for those who were receiving them, Employment Security Department. This government agency had a subdivision that was specifically assigned to provide employment services for those with disabilities. Steven was assigned two job coaches from this department, Doug B. and Cari M. Both were recent young college graduates and each of them had a different approach which was interesting for us to observe.

Cari was enthusiastic and outgoing. She approached the job search vigorously and aggressively; she was not to be deterred in finding Steven a job. She really enjoyed working with Steven, and we knew if there was a job out there for him, she would find it and get him placed into it.

Doug, by contrast, was very quiet and "laid back" in his approach, which was also good for Steven, as Doug helped Steven in maintaining a calm and relaxed attitude for learning any new skills that were required. This attitude was therefore very beneficial for Steven when he was making the adjustment to a new job.

This wonderful team of Cari and Doug stayed with Steven for about three or four years, but eventually all good things come to an end, and Cari reached the point where she wanted to make some personal changes in her life. She had saved enough money to quit the job and travel to India with friends for at least a year, and so we said good-bye to Cari, wishing her well in her new adventure, and continued with Doug. Steven knew Doug and worked well with him, so this disruption did not necessarily make a big difference until the time came when Steven lost a job and had to find a new one. This is when we really missed Cari with her enthusiasm for seeking out jobs and getting Steven hired. We always felt that we had to prod Doug a little more, and his communication with us as to progress was less forthcoming than Cari's, but he genuinely liked Steven nevertheless, and he eventually came through with a successful placement.

Steven worked with Doug for approximately ten more years before we received first a phone call and then a letter stating that this state agency was closing the department that covered the services being provided to Steven and that we would be required to find a new provider. And so closed a long chapter of Steven's life at work.

Over these years Steven moved in and out of numerous jobs as a dishwasher. Throughout the years sometimes we laughed at situations in the various jobs, sometimes we cried, sometimes we were angry, and sometimes we were astonished.

He worked in several different kinds of settings, but primarily in restaurants. The positive side of restaurant work is that there are usually plenty of openings, especially for dishwashers. The downside is that the hours are irregular which can make transportation arrangements challenging, and there is a high failure rate of restaurants which leads to significant job turnover. That in itself is a special problem for autistic people, as they have a more difficult time adjusting to change.

Several incidents stand out in regard to this turnover problem with restaurants. One of Steven's earliest and most successful jobs was with a large chain where he worked for one of the franchises. He stayed in this job for about five years, when all of a sudden, he was laid off. The reason, we learned, was that the franchise was sold to a new owner who was of Asian heritage and he employed only his own relatives, so the entire staff had been laid off. There were several other closures over the next few years, but another that stands out in memory is a restaurant that was going out of business but told no one. They continued to have the employees go to work and issued paychecks that were returned as insufficient funds. Needless to say, that job ended, and Steven was never paid for his last two weeks of work.

The closure that saddened us the most was one that has happened the most recently. Steven had been out of work for about six months during the time that there was a widespread recession. Dan P., a friend of ours came to us inquiring about rental space in one of our commercial buildings. He had just received a contract from friends of his who were restaurant owners to build the booths for a new restaurant that they were opening in nearby Silverdale. Dan had a limited budget and needed only a small space, so we offered to share a space with him that we were using ourselves as a workshop. Since he was sharing it with us, we were able to give him a generous discount on the rent.

In a conversation with him, we shared our concern about Steven's lack of a job in this poor economy, upon which he offered to talk to his friends about a job for Steven in their new restaurant. These owners also had a restaurant in Seattle, and had made it a point to hire some workers with disabilities. They were very generous, understanding and supportive, and they firmly believed in using their resources to help others in this way. Thus, they were very experienced in having employees with developmental disabilities.

Well, when Dan told them about Steven, they practically hired him "sight unseen". They met him first, of course, but when Steven went for the first meeting with them, they had the paperwork ready for him to sign and they already had him on the work schedule. This family-owned business was by far the most wonderful employer that Steven ever had. It took a few weeks to work out the transportation details; the Access bus dropped him off at the wrong place once or twice, and it sometimes had difficulty being on time to pick him up after work. The manager at the restaurant was especially conscientious about looking out for him, making phone calls to the appropriate people, to ensure that he got home safely after work.

The entire staff was so understanding and helpful when Steven was new and learning the routine of the job. The owners were also very generous in their compensation package; they included Steven in the tip pool and gave him a starting pay that was more than minimum wage. After we received the first several paychecks and reported them to Social Security, we realized that Steven was making too much money and it would jeopardize his eligibility for services. Since the most important aspect of having a job for Steven was the simple fact that he had a job and had something to do, and not how much money he made, we thanked the owners for being so generous, but explained to them that they needed to pay Steven less because we needed all of the services he received, including the job coach, the compensation for care at the group home, and his medical care.

The restaurant owners were also very happy with Steven's work performance. He is a good worker, tries very hard to please and is reliable about being on the job when expected. At one point, Holly Ridge, the job coach agency, had been contacted by our State Legislative Representative about visiting some work sites where they had clients placed that were a success. They immediately thought of Steven, so this restaurant and Steven became a part of the Legislator's tour and was highlighted as a success story.

Steven stayed at this job for five years, and was so happy there. It was in his final summer of working there that he had become so ill and spent the long two weeks in the hospital. He expressed two major concerns in the hospital; one was whether or not he would still be able to go on his vacation to Disney World in the winter, and the other was whether or not he would be able to return to his job. He kept telling us that he wanted to get better so that he could go back to work.

It was shortly after he returned to work however, that we learned the restaurant was not financially successful enough for the owners to stay open and that it would be closing within weeks. We were all so very sad; this was a blow to all of the employees who worked there, and so it was a loss to the entire community, not just Steven. Several weeks after the closure we received Steven's final paycheck in the mail, and to our great surprise a very generous bonus had been added to his check. I cannot say enough good things about the quality of the character of these employers. These are the kind of people who contribute so very much to the lives of others and give back so much to the community.

One of the things that we learned very early is that success on the job for Steven depended not only on the attitude of the person doing the hiring, but also on the attitudes of his co-workers. If he had a supportive employer but the other employees didn't accept him it was a prescription for failure. There are several examples of how the lack of support of co-workers led to failure for Steven. In one instance, Steven was working in a Nursing Home setting, and one employee in particular did not like Steven. Doug was his job coach at the time, and told us that one or two of the workers were complaining about having to work with Steven, so Steven was finally let go.

One of the complaints had been that Steven broke too many glasses and created an unsafe work environment for them. About a month later Steven was talking about the job to us and told us that "Dave" broke the glass at work. Steven volunteered this information without any prompting, and we were surprised because we had not discussed it with him at all.

Although Steven had made some minor attempts at deception when he was much younger, his attempts were very transparent and easily detected.   Autistic people generally don't tell lies because they do not know how. One of the biggest deficits in autism is the ability to think about abstract concepts, and being able to be deceptive requires this skill. Therefore, we know that Steven was telling us the truth; that the co-worker had in fact broken the glass and then placed the blame on Steven, knowing that Steven would be unable to defend himself. So this is an instance in which a co-worker blatantly used Steven's disability to harm Steven, and this is a direct type of abuse that very much angered us. However, it was in Steven's best interest to let it go and move on. We did not want him to be placed in a situation where he was disliked and used in this manner.

In another instance, there was some employee manipulation that led to a negative result for Steven, but this time it was not so blatantly apparent that he was being used. He was working in a hotel restaurant and the hours were often very late and very long. In this instance he got off work so late at night that the Access Bus was not available, and we had to hire a private taxi to take him home, sometimes as late as 2 A.M. Steven had been working at this restaurant for nearly two years when we started hearing about complaints through Doug. One complaint was that Steven was eating food off of the dishes that were being bused back for washing, especially the left-over desserts, as we later learned. But the main complaint was that when he finished work, sometimes at 2 A.M., it took 20 to 30 minutes for his taxi ride to arrive, and in the meantime he was in the lobby of the hotel riding the elevator up and down. This apparently caused some noise and distraction, especially at that hour. Without giving us a chance to try to rectify the situation by talking to the taxi company about a timely pick up, the restaurant decided to terminate his employment. Had Cari been the job coach at that time, I think there would have been a little more exploration of the problem and a discussion about some solutions before Steven was terminated; but Doug was not as aggressive nor did he act as a strong advocate, and so it became an unpreventable conclusion.

However, we later had to laugh because as I began to explore with Doug what had happened, we learned "the rest of the story". First of all, the previous manager had been replaced with a new manager who was not as understanding of Steven's limitations. Secondly, most employees really want to avoid the "closing" shift of a restaurant as much as possible. Well, Steven was actually doing a good job, and apparently some of the employees had talked the new manager into allowing Steven to take a number of the closing shifts on a consistent basis. When we heard this we were astonished, as Steven was there by himself to close and had been doing this for about six months! Closing requires multiple tasks, not just simply finishing the dishes; so he had been able to learn and process a much more complicated skill set than we would have imagined him being able to do without supervision. In addition he had done it successfully for some time. It was only when the taxi started being late that a problem surfaced. Steven has always loved elevators, and to this day he finds it difficult to pass by an elevator without first riding it up and down. So it was his obsession with elevators, and not his actual job performance that proved to be his undoing in this situation. And once more there had been employee manipulation in a situation where Steven was not able to defend himself; he simply accepted the undesirable shifts without comment because he didn't know any better.

In another of Steven's jobs, he did have multiple tasks which he was able to learn with rote memorization and could perform very well as long as there was no spontaneous deviation from the memorized tasks required. However, one day there was a coffee pot which had been left on by someone else inadvertently, and it was boiling over. Since minding the coffee pot was not one of Steven's delineated tasks, he walked right by it without blinking an eye and paid no attention to the fact that it was making a mess. Another employee apparently knew that Steven had been the last person in the room prior to the discovery of the coffee pot boiling over and this person was really upset that Steven had not taken care of the issue. The co-worker had a very obvious lack of understanding about the functioning of an autistic person. He apparently felt that Steven had willfully ignored the coffee pot because he was too lazy to deal with it. Once again, Doug was a weak advocate for Steven, and Steven was terminated before we even had knowledge of the situation. However, we felt that with such a huge lack of understanding of the disability, that it would never be a successful placement anyway, and perhaps this is also how Doug was looking at the situation. In any case, we did have to smile at this situation, as it was such a classic demonstration of an autistic characteristic.

Probably one of the most significant obstacles for a person with a disability to overcome in obtaining employment is finding adequate transportation. Years before, when Kitsap County was in the earliest stages of developing its bus transportation system, I had attended meetings with my friend, Jean W., and we had advocated for the special transportation system to take people with disabilities to their jobs who otherwise would be unable to work. With the help of others who supplied services to the developmentally disabled, our county was convinced that the service was needed and they decided to provide it.

At the outset, it was instituted specifically for this one intended purpose, but as governmental agencies are wont to do, they discovered that the service could receive more funding if it was expanded to provide rides to seniors for reasons such as doctor appointments and shopping trips. We did not take exception to this, as helping seniors be as independent as possible for as long as possible is certainly a legitimate cause. The problem arose when the mission for seniors took priority over that of getting disabled people to their jobs. Over time it seemed that the county forgot that the original mission was to get our disabled people to a job, and the doctor appointments started to take first priority. The window for pick up and drop off times for our disabled clients became larger and larger, and soon we found that Steven was getting to work as much as an hour before time, and waiting after work for just as long. The days and hours of available bus service also began to meet the needs of the seniors more than the work days and hours of the clients with disabilities. The doctor appointments for seniors coincided better with regular 9-5 hours, 5 days per week for the bus employees, instead of the late hours and weekend and holidays that low end wage scale workers face on their jobs. We know that Steven lost at least two jobs due to this transportation problem with the large time window for drop off and pick up. Although he tries very hard to do what is expected of him, an hour of sitting or standing outside the door of his place of work waiting for the bus to arrive is simply too much time. That is when he became bored and found things to do that were more interesting to him, but less acceptable to others, such as riding the elevator in the hotel lobby.

Probably the most distressing situation regarding transportation for work occurred on an Easter Sunday. The bus was not running that day, so a taxi was called to take Steven to work. However, the restaurant was also closed on that day, which Steven knew, but apparently it had not been communicated adequately to the group home. This was at the time that Steven was in Nancy's group home, and she was very ill, so was not as "on top of things" as would normally be expected. At any rate, the taxi arrived to pick up Steven at the usual time for his Sunday work schedule. His job at the time was at a restaurant located in a shopping center, so the taxi dropped him off at the usual place just outside of the shopping center without noticing the fact that the shopping center was totally closed.

Early afternoon arrived, and Phil and I received a phone call from the group home that Steven was missing. The story was that James, Nancy's son who was helping with the care at the home, noticed that Steven was not around and had just assumed that he was in his room sleeping. When he looked in the room it was empty so they started making phone calls and realized that Steven had been taken to work hours ago, but that nothing was open and no one knew where he was.

Phil jumped in the car to go to the shopping center to look for him, about a 45-minute drive from where we live. I stayed home by the phone in case anyone found him and tried to call us. James also went to the shopping center and Nancy stayed at the group home in case of a phone call. Neither Phil nor James were able to locate him, so the Sheriff's Office was called in on the search. Ironically, Steven had a cell phone which we had given him for just such an emergency and he knew how to use it, but he didn't leave it on because as he explained to me, that would be "wasting battery".

After about an hour of searching with several "Steven sightings" reported, he was finally located calmly waiting at his pick up spot at the end of what would have been his work shift, waiting for the taxi to come and take him home. Apparently, after he was dropped off and discovered that the restaurant was closed, he decided to walk to an adjacent shopping center where a few stores were open and do a little shopping. He always carries some money in his wallet, so he purchased some small food items, then enjoyed the freedom of just walking around on his own and window shopping. When it was time for the taxi to pick him up, he returned to his place in front of the restaurant and waited. We were all very relieved, but this was also a demonstration that Steven can function quite well when left to his own devices, and that sometimes we do not give him enough credit for being able to do some things when he is actually quite capable. We were not worried that he would run away or get lost, but our major concern was that some unsavory person might pick him up and hurt him, as he is very innocent in this regard.


## SEXUALITY

Another topic that is more sensitive, but that nevertheless must be addressed by all parents of adult children with developmental disabilities is sexual behavior. In so many ways these children are no different than our normal children; they are not sexually neutral. As they grow and develop they experience sexual feelings and emotions, just like everyone. With our normal children we teach them about acceptable behavior and attitudes as we go along and as they appear to be ready to learn. Therein lies the rub with our developmentally delayed/disabled children. Autistic children in particular present an especially challenging picture as far as knowing when they are ready to learn about sexual matters due to their specific communication deficits and their often perplexing behavior.

Steven, in particular, did not know how to express his feelings to us. Even though he always seemed to understand most of what we said to him, his expressive language disorder prevented him from being able to tell us his thoughts and feelings. Therefore, our challenge was to decipher his feelings and thoughts through observation of his behavior. The other challenge that parents of autistic children in particular face is that these children tend to learn a behavior and then focus on it, repeating it over and over, even when it is an inappropriate one. They also focus on a particular topic of conversation and then repeat that over and over, even in socially unacceptable circumstances, as they are unable to differentiate when a behavior or a conversation is socially acceptable to others, and when it is not.

I am including this topic here because it had a profound effect on Steven's ability to keep his latest job, and then his ability to obtain a new one. When he was a baby and toddler he rejected being held and cuddled, almost as if it was physically painful for him. As he progressed to elementary school age it became apparent that he was attracted to adults of the opposite sex, as he exhibited a special attraction to certain female teachers, seeking out their attention and hugs. That seemed normal to us and we were happy to see him begin to appreciate the showing and receiving of affection to and from others.

When he reached high school age we did not notice an appreciable difference in how he related to females with certain exceptions. The exceptions were that he developed a strong attachment to me, and also to one or two specific teachers. So when we at one time cherished the hugs, we now realized that we would need to control this physical expression of affection; he was now a young adult and we would need to teach him that prolonged hugging and kissing was not appropriate. At this point in time he was not able to "self limit", and so we had to limit for him by telling him he could no longer give hugs to me or to other adult women. With the advice and agreement of the school staff we proceeded in this manner and it seemed to resolve the issue for a long time until Steven entered the workplace. It was then that the behavior of inappropriate hugging and kissing resurfaced. He developed an attraction for one of the waitresses at work and fortunately she was understanding. With the help of the job coach, and the supportive discussion with us about the fact that he could not hug anyone at work or he would lose his job, he seemed to understand and continued in that job without incident.

There were continued issues however; when Steven felt aroused he would put his hands in his pockets and self-stimulate whether or not he was in public. I learned that whenever we were with Steven I needed to wear long jeans because bare legs were stimulating to him. The behavior was not constant but it was frequent enough that we found ourselves reminding him to "be careful where he put his hands, and to remove them from his pocket". Once more, we found it difficult to know how to communicate with him on this matter, and instead of trying to enter into complicated conversations with him about sex, we decided to simply attempt to modify his behavior. We had no control over the situation when he was not with us, so we assumed that unless we received negative feedback that he was managing adequately in other situations.

Our complacence came to a screeching halt when we received a phone call from Steven's most recent job coach, Brittani. In his prior job he had worked for five years without incident regarding sexual conduct and his reason for leaving this job was that the restaurant closed. He then started work at another nearby restaurant which was a large national chain. We were so delighted with this placement; it was close to where he lived, the employees and management all seemed to be so supportive, and it was a popular location making it unlikely that it would close any time soon. We were looking forward to Steven finally being able to enjoy a longterm, stable job situation. So Brittani's phone call on that sunny afternoon came as a bolt of lightning jolting us out of our relaxed complacence about Steven's current situation. Brittani told us that he had lost his job and that he had been dismissed almost on the spot following a behavior incident.

In the immediate aftermath, even Brittani was not sure what had happened, but as we were able to piece it together over the next several days, this is what we found out: Steven was at the end of his work shift and was waiting outside in front of the restaurant for his bus to pick him up and take him home. He was still wearing his uniform that identified him as an employee of the restaurant. He had been waiting for a long time and was apparently getting restless and bored, so he put his hands in his pocket and started self-stimulating, not vigorously, but noticeably. A female customer was either entering or leaving the restaurant, and Steven caught her attention. She became extremely upset, asking to see the manager right away, and proceeded to loudly voice her complaint about Steven to the manager. Because Steven's physical appearance is so normal, we are certain that she thought he was a dangerous sex offender, perhaps even a pedophile, and she would have had no idea that Steven did not understand the gravity of his behavior in this very public setting, and that he was not dangerous.

We took immediate action to mitigate and prevent further repercussions from this incident, but it has led all of us down a difficult road. It is critical that Steven either has a job, or that he has some other productive activities, otherwise he simply sits around doing nothing or lying in bed all day and all night. The first step we took was to be honest with Steven and tell him that he lost his job because he did inappropriate touching of his penis in a public place. We then explained to him that it was okay to do that in privacy, such as in the bathroom or his bedroom at home, but that he should never ever do it again in a public setting. We emphasized again that when he was in public he must always keep his hands at his sides. Well, he is smart enough, and he was upset enough about losing the job that he definitely understood what we were telling him. He has a strong desire to please and to do what is expected of him, so we were fairly certain that there would not be a repeat performance in the future. But we decided that due to the gravity of the situation we needed to take additional steps, so I located an adult autism center at the University of Washington in Seattle and made an appointment for Steven and myself.

We had a meeting with an extremely knowledgeable nurse practitioner who was in charge of the clinic and had many years of experience working with autistic children and adults. She re-assured me that Steven's behavior was very common and normal for autistic adults and after talking to Steven, she agreed with me that he did in fact understand the difference between public and private behavioral standards. I had requested medication as an additional insurance for the future  but the meds I had read about that had been used for this purpose had some very bad side effects. She felt that these stronger medications would not be warranted for Steven, but there was a milder  prescription that had few if any side effects and which she felt would be helpful in blunting some of the strong sexual desire and help him have more control over that part of his life.

We also met with the caregivers of the group home and asked them to help us reinforce appropriate behavior when he was at home with them too. Our other concern was whether or not re-ports from this last job would follow him forward, making it im-possible for him to get another job. Therefore, I went and talked to the manager of the restaurant and tried to clarify what had actually happened and what we could expect as far as what they would report to a future employer. He was very nice and very articulate; he liked Steven and said that Steven had been an excel-lent worker. He felt that the customer complaint was an over-re-action on her part, but that they had no choice but to take action and let Steven go. He said that if asked about Steven, they would simply report that his job performance was good. He even volunteered that he would give him a good reference, but I did not pursue that, as I felt that he had given me adequate assurance that they would not blackball Steven for future employers.

The owner of the group home also had some good suggestions for the future which I shared with Brittani, the job coach. He suggested that Steven's contact with customers could be limited by finding a drop off and pick up location at a back door rather than the front entrance i.e., at the employee entrance if there is one. We also both agreed that the long wait time for transportation on either end was not an acceptable situation for any person with a disability, and that we would find private transportation and pay for it if necessary.

After having taken all of these measures to mitigate the undesirable occurrence from happening again we felt that it was time to move forward and actively seek a new job for Steven. However, we have found that this is more easily said than done. Shortly after Steven was dismissed from the job, Brittani left the agency where she worked as Steven's job coach in order to go back to school and a new job coach was assigned. Steven was also referred back to the Department of Vocational Rehabilitation since they provide the funding for job training, and there was someone new on the job as his caseworker there as well. So it seemed like we were starting all over from the beginning with a first job and so far we have had zero success. As I am writing this, Steven has been unemployed for 10 months and we are still waiting to receive a report that a new job has been found for Steven.

For Steven the importance of having a job is the same as it is for anyone else. It not only provides something for him to do other than staying in bed and sleeping all day, but it also gives him a sense of worth. He loves to work and he loves to earn money. He keeps track of his earnings and saves money to go on outings and to shop for food treats that he especially likes to eat.

He is also quite generous; he is very tuned in to the birthdays of all immediate family members and carefully remembers to buy a gift for each of us. He has always been very excited about Christmas, and also buys everyone a Christmas gift. We always smile about Steven at Christmas. He gives us his list, then makes sure to ask whether we went to the store before Christmas to buy everything on the list. Then as soon as the presents are all wrapped and under the tree, he checks them all to count how many are for him and knows exactly where they are under the tree. On Christmas morning he passes out all of the gifts and is careful to make sure that he gives each of us a gift in turn, opening his each time only when everyone else has opened theirs in turn.

Through having a job and earning his own money, he has learned the importance of giving to others, and this also contributes to his sense of worth and well being.

*Steven at work at the Silverdale Hotel - summer 1997*

Hi Cyndi & Phil ☺                                    2/4/00

Doug came across these photos he
took back in 1997. I thought they
were great & you guys might like the
~~copy~~ copies.
                    Take Care,
                              Cari
PS  I don't think
    Steven has gotten to see
             them yet either.

*A note from job coach Cari.*

**Dear Geoffrey Thank You for the Coke Piggy Bank for My Christmas for Put
Moneys into Coke Piggy Bank for Eat Dinner Out at Chainise Restuarants at
Epcopt Center in Florida and Eat Dinner Out at Germeny Restuarants at
Epcop Center in Florida and Two Days of Eat Dinner Out at Sarastoga
Spring Resort Hotel Restuarants has Bacon Cheese Burger with French
Fries at Sarastoga Spring Resort Hotel Restuarants in Florida and include
Two Days of Typhoon Lagoon Water Slide in Florida**

**Love: Steven Rasmussen**

*Thank you not for a Christmas gift - 2012.*

# THE BIG TRIPS

From the time the children were quite small we recognized that all of us needed a break from the daily routine once in a while, so we established a tradition of taking at least an annual trip. We didn't have much money in the beginning and in addition, staying in motels and eating out in restaurants was not a friendly venue for our family given the problems with Steven's behavior. We solved these problems by purchasing a tent trailer that contained small kitchen camping facilities and sleeping quarters for everyone. The children loved "camping out"; the vacation was affordable, and we weren't disturbing sleeping guests in the room next door of a motel if Steven decided to throw a temper tantrum in the middle of the night.

From the time he was a small child, Steven was strongly attracted to activities that provided certain types of sensory input. He seemed to crave the motion created by going up and down in elevators or riding in roller coasters. He was also fascinated by water, and could spend hours pouring water back and forth from one container to another, watching the flow. He jumped up and down in delight when he saw waterfalls, and he absolutely loved going on waterslides. So as he grew older, we started planning trips that included visits to amusement or waterslide parks. One of our early trips was to Disneyland in California, staying in a nearby campground in the tent trailer. This was a delightful trip for all of the children. When Steven was finished with school and had a job he began saving his money for an annual vacation trip.

One of the first trips that he planned and saved for was a trip with Dad to Disney World in Florida. At the time, I was running my own business as a real estate appraiser, and Geoffrey was still at home going to school, so I needed to stay home and Phil got the honors of taking the trip with Steven. It was a huge success and turned into an annual event. After a few years, I was able to go too, and on one of the trips we came across an exhibit at the park where timeshares were being sold. Realizing that taking Steven to Disney World was probably going to be a long term commitment, it seemed like a financially feasible investment to buy this timeshare and it has turned out to be something we have never regretted. Steven planned his "Big Trip" to Disney World every year, saving his money, deciding which resort we would stay in and giving us a long list of all of the rides he wanted to do each day of our visit. He knows how to type on the computer and has this list all typed out for us when we go.

For many years his "Big Trip" plans were for Disney World every year, but as he has gotten older he has become more flexible and has actually decided that he wanted to vary the routine. Some of the years he now chooses Las Vegas, where he enjoys many of the rides at the various casinos, as well as swimming in the beautiful casino swimming pools. Several years ago he decided he wanted to go to Hawaii to visit Disney's Aulani Resort, which is mainly a waterslide park. We have also taken him to waterslides in Canada in the summer, and weekend trips to Victoria, Canada where we visit Butchart Gardens and go to the large Museum of Natural History located there.

Some of the most enjoyable times we have spent with Steven are on these trips and it is such a joy for us to see him earning his money and being able to enjoy spending it just as our normal children would do. It reinforces for us that all of the effort and difficult times we went through for so many years have been worth it; that this child too can have a happy and productive life.

Saturday March 13th Visit Sandy Hook House
Sunday March 14th Take the Seattle Ferry Boat to Seattle Airport for Ride in Extra Elevator at One Time and Inside Seattle Airport for Get in Lines for the Security at Inside Seattle Airport and Leave Seattle and Arrive Tampa
Sunday March 14th One Night at Motel Six in Tampa
Monday March 15th Find Rooms at Disney's Wilderness Lodge Resort Hotel
Monday March 15th Disney's Typhoon Lagoon Water Slide in the After Noon
Monday March 15th Disney's MGM Studio at Night
Monday March 15th Water Slide at Disney's Wilderness Lodge Resort Hotel and Night
Tuesday March 16th Magic Kingdom Walt Disney's World Rides in the Morning and at After Noon
Tuesday March 16th Epcopt Center Rides at Night
Wednesday March 17th Disney's Typhoon Lagoon Water Slide in the Morning
Wednesday March 17th Epcopt Center Rides in the After Noon and at Night
Thursday March 18th Magic Kingdom Walt Disney's World Rides in the Morning
Thursday March 18th Epcopt Center Rides in the After Noon and at Night
Thursday March 18th One Night at Motel Six in Tampa
Friday March 19th Leave Tampa and Arrive Seattle

*Steven's agenda for the trip to Disney World - approximately 2000*

*Phil And Boys With Camper*

*Boys Hiking In Olympic Mountains*

*Steven at Victoria, Canada.*

*(l.) Steven Geoff and dad at Dungeness Spit.*

*(r.) Steven riding a bike at the Southern California beach trip.*

*Family Reunion Yellowstone, 1988.*

*Mt. Whistler, Canada, 1990.*

*Steven at the Tacoma Zoo.*

# NAVIGATING THE SYSTEM:
# A TANGLED WEB

One of the most confusing and frustrating things for parents of a special needs child is learning to navigate the way through the bureaucratic red tape in order to receive Federal and State services for their child. It is akin to traveling through a never-ending obstacle course; and of all people, I should have been better prepared.

Two examples from my earlier experiences stand out in my memory. The first dates from the time when Phil and I were first married and he was a young officer in the Navy. At one point in his career he was responsible for submitting a budget request for the upcoming annual funding of a project. He conscientiously looked for some cost saving cuts in order to have a reduced budget for the next year. He was immediately reprimanded and told that you should NEVER ask for a reduced budget, that the goal was always to ask for more money than you needed so that the budget was constantly increased. At the time, we were astounded by this philosophy of budgeting that we now know is standard "bureaucratic think". It is not necessary for actions to make sense; there is simply a way that things are always done, and whether or not it makes sense is not important. What is important is keeping your job and this means no deviation from the rules, whatever they are at the time.

The second example is an incident from my days as a caseworker at the San Diego County Department of Public Welfare. Part of my caseload consisted of cases known as AFDC-U (Aid to Families with Dependent Children-Unemployed Fathers in the home). In this particular case there was a mother with 12 children in the home. There were six to eight different fathers, but the last two children had been fathered by the man who was living in the home at the time. He was employed as a brick layer but didn't make quite enough money to support all 12 of the children, so the family was eligible for extra assistance. There was a problem, however, due to the fact that he also had another family with two children from a previous relationship, and this mother was required to seek support from him in order for her to be eligible for assistance. Since he wasn't paying support to her, she had to report him to the District Attorney's office and he was arrested. While he was in jail he lost his job, so now there were 14 children who were being totally supported by the Welfare Department. When the father finally was released from jail, he tried to go back to his previous well-paying job as a brick layer but was unable to do so because his union dues had lapsed. He needed a nominal sum that was well within the ability of the Department to provide, but he had no way of procuring it without a job.

When I received this case, I tried "every which way but up" to find a way to budget the amount to pay the dues but I was unsuccessful, so we continued to pay for all 14 children to be on public assistance. What a travesty, and all due to bureaucratic red tape from inflexible rules that made no sense whatsoever.

With this background I had thought it would be reasonable to assume that procuring services for Steven through the various governmental and private agencies would be a simple task; however, this has been far from the case and I have found it a continuing struggle to keep up with the rules and the changes in rules for ongoing services. It is like a moving target; just when I think I understand what needs to be done, I am informed that everything has changed, and I am forced to adjust and start over in order to maintain eligibility for Steven for the services he needs.

In the beginning, it did not seem to be so difficult. After Steven was diagnosed conclusively at the UCLA Neuropsychiatric Clinic as having autism, we were referred to the San Diego County Regional Center, a department of the state of California that provided the services for people with developmental disabilities. This state agency then provided the funding for Steven to attend the Los Niños Center until we moved to Washington, where he attended the public schools.

After Steven turned 18, there were two major changes regarding his legal status. He was now legally an adult and no longer considered to be our dependent child. This meant that his eligibility for services no longer was determined by our financial resources and since he was permanently disabled he was eligible for Social Security Supplemental Income. He was also eligible for state-provided medical care, called Medicaid. Since he was still living in our home and attending the public school, he did not immediately receive the social security income, but it became available to him as soon as he moved out of our home and into the first group home.

The second major change involved his legal status as an adult. Even though he was legally an adult, he was clearly disabled in terms of being able to make decisions on his own, manage his money, make medical decisions and live by himself. He needed the protection of a legal guardian or guardians, so Phil and I went through the process of applying to the Court and being granted legal guardianship of Steven when he turned 18. It is always preferable for this to be done by a close family member or members. No one loves this child more than the parents, or the adult siblings if parents are no longer able.

The last resort would be to allow the state to make decisions regarding the care of your loved one. Decisions made by the state agency typically are made in the best interest of the agency and not your child, and this fact has been brought home to me more than once over the years. A striking example of this was when one of Steven's group homes was closed and the agency tried to move him out of our county. He would have lost his job that he loved and where he had been working for nearly five years had I not had the legal right to intervene. I insisted that a placement be found where he would have transportation and could keep his job.

Maintaining eligibility for services is one of the most aggravating aspects of dealing with the bureaucracy. The Social Security Supplemental Income program is means tested, and Steven was eligible as long as he was disabled and had no income over a certain level, as well as no assets worth more than $2,000. When he was 21 and started working, he remained eligible for SSI as long as his income did not exceed a certain level. I was required to report Steven's income on a monthly basis by submitting his original pay stubs to the local office. I also had to submit evidence of any work-related expenses, such as his transportation costs. These documents were returned to me after being recorded in the Social Security records.

This continued for years, and at first I discarded my records after three years. I needed them until then for preparing my tri-annual report for the Court in order to maintain our guardianship status. We also had to return an annual report to Social Security regarding Steven's income and expenses from that source. Then, about five years after he started working, I received a notice from Social Security that they needed to have me re-submit all of his pay stubs and expense reports for the last five years. Since I had already discarded at least two of those years, I was frantic about maintaining his eligibility. So I made an appointment with the local office, only to learn that I was dealing with two local offices. As the legal guardian, I was also Steven's Representative Payee, so everything was always mailed to me where we lived, which was Jefferson County. Steven, however, lived and worked in Kitsap County, so the pay-stubs had all been mailed to the Kitsap County office and recorded in that office. The two offices did not talk to each other, so now the Jefferson County office wanted all of the information for the last five years that had already been submitted to the Kitsap County office. After my appointment, the two offices were finally able to resolve the issue, and I submitted the pay-stubs to both offices going forward.

About two years ago, I received another letter, this time from the national Social Security Office, requesting 10 years of back pay-stubs and work receipts. I was flabbergasted that this was happening again, but this time I had the records. I boxed them all up in a cardboard file box and mailed them with a letter requesting the return of the documents so I would have them the next time I received such a request. I never heard back regarding this request, and the box was never returned. I suspect that the box was opened, someone glanced at it, then checked off a space in the paperwork marked "documents received" and sent it to the shredder or trash can.

When Steven had been working about ten years, there was another major Social Security snafu. Out of the blue I received a letter stating that he was no longer eligible for SSI because he had been working and paying into the Disability program. Once more panic set in; what on earth were they talking about? All of Steven's services were tied into his eligibility for Social Security. We paid his room and board at the group home from his Social Security check, and the group home also received a substantial sum from the State DSHS for his caregivers in the home. His job coach was also paid for by DSHS, as was his medical care. We really could not afford for him to lose eligibility.

After making numerous phone calls and being placed on hold for hours, I was finally able to get to the bottom of the situation. It seems that Social Security has numerous computers to track programs and the people in them receiving the services. At some point the computers came up with the information that Steven had paid enough into the system from deductions made from his paychecks the last 10 years or so that he was eligible for regular Social Security Disability, or SDI. This program is based solely on the ongoing disability of the person, and the amount of earned income that is less than a certain level. Steven met both of these requirements and had been changed from SSI to SDI. He would have received more money from SDI than he received from SSI, and therefore was entitled to a lump sum payment for the difference between the two programs dating from the time he was first eligible for SDI. However, in typical fashion for a large governmental agency, it took five more years for it to determine the amount of the lump sum. In the meantime he was terminated from SSI and started receiving SDI. I was not worried about the lump sum payment, my only concern was that his eligibility be continued so that he wouldn't lose all of his services.

Five years later, when the lump sum check arrived, we were once more astounded. The amount was well over $20,000 and this presented a new dilemma for us. I called the attorney that represents us in the Guardianship and asked him what we should do with the money. He told us what we already knew, that it could only be spent for Steven's needs, and said the best thing to do with it would be to put it into an interest-bearing trust account in Steven's name and use it over time as needed for Steven. We had to have this approved by the Court, which was done.

About two years later we received another eligibility review request, this time from DSHS. The form asked for a list of all bank accounts in Steven's name, which I dutifully filled out and returned. Shortly thereafter I received a panic call from a DSHS representative asking me lots of questions about the trust account. I explained that it was money received from Social Security as a lump sum and that we had put it into an account as required by the Court, to be used for Steven's needs. She responded that we had 18 months in which to expend any such lump sum payments, and after that they would effect ongoing eligibility. I asked her what to do to remedy the situation, and she was able to find the buried section of the State law that told us how to handle it. I passed this information on to our attorney, who then reworded the terms of the Trust and had that approved by the Court. We then needed to put the bank account in my name so that Steven would never have direct access to it. The terms of the Trust also stated that when Steven passed away, any monies remaining in the Trust would revert to the State.

We have always been grateful to this state employee who went out of her way to help us resolve a sticky issue which could have had disastrous consequences for us and Steven. This is, however, another example of the conflicting rules and regulations that we are trying to follow and despite our best efforts we still find ourselves out of compliance and in jeopardy of losing services for Steven. The saving grace is that most of the people with whom we have had direct contact are dedicated and sincerely interested in doing everything they can to meet the needs of the population they are serving. Without the help of many of our caseworkers along the way we would never have been able to come as far as we have with helping Steven to have a good life. We are forever grateful to these good people, and we would encourage other parents to work with them and let them know how much they are appreciated.

I have spent hundreds of hours over the years preparing financial reports for the Court and for the various agencies, conducting interviews with them and waiting on the phone for answers to problems that I have been unable to unravel. I am a college graduate, a former caseworker for a state agency where I was in charge of determining eligibility for my caseload, a bookkeeper, and a former real estate appraiser who worked with facts and figures for banks for 20 years, yet I am constantly having difficulties understanding the rules and requirements of the various agencies. I have come to the conclusion that it is a moving target and a tangled web that no one really understands.

I do have great concerns about having to leave this problem to our sons who will take over Guardianship of Steven when we are no longer able to do it; but my advice to them is to find an attorney who specializes in serving the needs of the disabled to help them. It is our plan to leave enough money in a trust for Steven that this need can be met.

# PART IV

## THE FAMILY

# IN DAD'S OWN WORDS

I am the Dad. During Steven's early years I spent my time working. Sometimes 12 hours a day and seven days a week. I was my own boss, building houses and always trying to meet some deadline or other. Finally Cindy told me I had to stop working on Sundays. Best thing that ever happened. This was so we could spend some time as a family and have fun with the kids.

And we did have fun. We joined the San Diego Zoological Society and went to the zoo just about every Sunday. Mark went to see the animals and Steven went to see the water. He was obsessed with water. We tried to get him interested in the animals, asking him what color each animal was so we could be sure that he was actually looking at the animal and not the water. We even made him repeat the name of the animal, such as "bear" or "giraffe", but this was a lost cause. He could repeat the sound, but when we came back later to ask him the name it was always "animan". However, he loved the streams of water that ran through the park.

Another activity we enjoyed was what we called "bathtub boats". Naturally, since it involved water, Steven loved it. We found a resort in Mission Bay called Vacation Village. They had small sailboats for rent that were just big enough to accommodate me and the two kids. These were our "bathtub boats". The lady who ran the concession got to know us and knew what we wanted each time we showed up. We would sail around the bay for a couple of hours, aimlessly, and go home satisfied with our Sunday outing.

After we moved up the coast to Solana Beach, Steven's interest turned to swimming pools. He had an uncanny sense about where they were and was always trying to escape to find one. After some fairly scary episodes, we decided that since he was so interested in water he had better learn how to swim. Cindy took him to have some lessons, and we were able to join a nearby tennis club that had a very small swimming pool. This pool was perfect for Steven to learn to swim. He did not respond very well to verbal instruction but after splashing around for a while he figured out how to get from one side of the pool to the other with something that resembled a dog paddle. After that, he was off and running, or swimming. He has never gotten past the dog paddle, and he can swim for hours, even in the San Diego surf. Now, when we go swimming together he worries about me more than I worry about him, and I am a very good swimmer.

After some years in Solana Beach, we moved up to Washington. On the way we spent some time at Mammoth Mountain and I endeavored to teach Mark and Steven to ski. Mark loved it and became a better skier than me. After we moved to Washington State, I volunteered to be a chaperone with the high school ski club, and was able to take Steven along. Ironically, the name of the ski resort is "Steven's Pass". Teaching Steven to ski was a bit of a struggle. Eventually he learned to ride the ski lift and make downhill turns, but it was never his favorite thing to do.

When we were looking for a place to build a home in Washington we passed up a view of the sun setting over Liberty Bay and the Olympic Mountains, and bought six acres of land so Steven could have some room to run. We also bought our own little sailing dinghy. It was a little bigger than the "bathtub boats" and would also accommodate the dog. Max was a black lab who also loved the water. The property fronted on Puget Sound so it was very convenient to use the boat. I would take one or both kids out and Max would just jump in and out of the boat as he pleased.

Max was Steven's constant companion and seemed to have a special sense about protecting him. In addition to the dog we also had, in succession, pigs, a goat, a pony, a horse and some llamas. Steven pretty much ignored the animals except the horse which he loved to "ride". Really what he did was sit on the horse bareback while "Miss Red" grazed. Like Max, Miss Red seemed to have a sixth sense about Steven and was quite comfortable to have him on her back.

We still had the tradition of doing "something fun" each weekend. Sometimes it was as simple as going to the mall and riding elevators and escalators. We also discovered the Tacoma Zoo, which has an aquarium. Steven's favorite exhibit at the zoo became "rocky shores" which displays walrus, Beluga whales, and sea otters. It has several levels connected by a handicapped elevator. For Steven this was heaven because it offered a combination of water and elevators, never mind the animals.

Another activity we enjoyed was riding the ferry to Seattle, ascending the hill to Fourth Avenue, taking the free bus to Westlake Center, and then the monorail to Seattle Center and back, riding some elevators downtown and working our way down through Pike Place Market and back to the ferry along the waterfront. The interesting thing about this route is that Steven showed me a way to do the whole thing without walking up the hill or taking any stairs. Somehow, he knew where to find all the elevators and escalators.

Even more than the zoo, Steven loved the waterslide park. It was located about two hours away in Issaquah, so we had to take a ferry and drive through Seattle to get there, but Steven was in heaven each time we went. Then about two years later they closed the park. Steven was despondent wondering what happened to it. We were finally able to explain that, "The man put it in a truck," and he still uses that expression to explain things that are gone. After that we had to take him up to Canada to use the waterslides there, which was inconvenient but okay since he loved it so much. Then a few years later, another waterslide park opened just south of Seattle and going there is still an annual event for us.

Steven's older brother, Mark, loves to hike in the outdoors, and some of the best hiking in the world is in the Olympic National Park which is practically at our back door. After Mark and I had explored a bit, it seemed like a good idea to invite Steven, who was about ten years old at the time, along on a three-day backpacking trip. He was excited to go and we got all outfitted up with backpacks, tents, food, and all of the usual paraphernalia. We set out and completed the loop around Seven Lakes Basin which took us above the tree line and out into the wilderness. During the trek he was a super trooper but when we got back home Steven really summed up the trip. He said, "The back hurt, the foot hurt, the arm hurt, the leg hurt, etc." Maybe he was just more honest than the rest of us but he has not expressed much interest in hiking since that trip. Mark, on the other hand, has gone on to explore the Sierra Nevada, the Cascades, and the upper Himalaya.

Amusement parks are another passion of Steven's. When we still lived in San Diego we had occasion to take the kids up to Anaheim to visit Disneyland and Knotts Berry Farm. Steven naturally loved the rides that involved water such as the submarine ride at Disney and the log ride at Knotts, but he also developed a taste for roller coaster type rides. Fortunately, I like these rides too, so I was able to be his partner.

After we moved up north, we still found occasion to go back to Anaheim and also added Magic Mountain. The roller coasters at Magic Mountain were almost too much for me but Steven never got tired of them, the bigger the better. Then we found out that Las Vegas also had several roller coasters and a water slide on the Strip, along with cheaper rooms and all-you-can-eat buffets.

One of the more memorable experiences we had in Las Vegas was the roller coaster on top of the Stratosphere Hotel. We got to sit in the front row because, unlike every other roller coaster, nobody else wanted it. But I thought the ride that shot you up the needle on the very top was even more heart pounding. We did that one too.

Going to Las Vegas has gotten more expensive since then, and the waterslide went away "on the truck".

Then I had occasion to attend a convention in Orlando. It took place in a very nice Marriott Hotel just across the freeway from Disney World. I decided that the next family trip should be Disney World, and we did come back a few months later. Steven loved it more than anyone, especially when we discovered that there were three water slides on the property ( one of them has since been "put on a truck"). Sometimes we all went together but Cindy was really busy with her appraisal business so I had the honor of taking Steven back to his new favorite place. After about four more trips I noticed that there was a "Disney Vacation Club" timeshare that we could join and get better accommodations. Since then Disney World has been an annual event.

Steven has always been my willing helper. He is always interested in my various building projects and is quite good at the non-verbal communication that takes place when carrying things or putting them into position. The first project that I remember his helping with was building a little rental house near the back (near the road) of our six acres in Washington. He is quite strong for his size and has absolutely no fear of heights. This is valuable when framing a roof. Except for hiring an electrician, Steven and I built this house all by ourselves. Since then he has been an enthusiastic helper with many building projects, and he expects, and gets, payment for his services which he saves for his "trips". He especially likes to "stir" concrete and help his dad hang drywall.

He also likes gardening. This is good because keeping him busy when he comes to visit from his group home is a challenge. There is usually some kind of gardening job to do. Although we left most of our six acres as natural woods, there were a couple of cleared areas where we planted grass. Together they were well over an acre, so it became apparent that we needed a riding lawnmower. Naturally, like all little boys, Steven was fascinated and wanted to drive. With some trepidation we let him try it, and he did okay. But he did not go back and forth as you must do to mow the lawn. He just drove randomly. I kept insisting that he "do it right" and after much guidance he finally got the idea. So now he likes to mow the lawn. He also has gotten quite good at knowing what is a weed and what is not, so now he helps at his group home as well. Last Christmas, his wish list mainly consisted of various gardening tools.

This brings us to the present. Steven still loves sailboats and we now have a large new sailboat. Sometimes I am able to go sailing with just the two of us. He likes to take the helm but he does a lousy job; despite my best efforts he cannot maintain anything like a straight course. I keep telling him to "do it right" as I did with the lawnmower and he still doesn't get it, but he loves to steer anyway. One of our plans has been to take an overnight trip down the Sound. Maybe this summer.

This winter we went out for a short jaunt on our recently acquired powerboat in Florida and he was all smiles. We went up the ICW with some friends to have lunch at a waterside restaurant. When we got back he told his mom that he did a good job of "acting normal" and he had.

Steven especially likes to do things on his own, where he can be "big". When I pick him up for a weekend at our home, the first thing he wants to do is stop at MacDonald's where he heads straight for the order desk to place his order by himself. Usually the workers are able to understand what he wants and they are always helpful. I do not interfere unless he has trouble placing the order because I, and usually the clerk, understand that this is his way of functioning as a normal person, or "being big".

I also feel that this is one of the reasons he likes waterslides so much. After we arrive at the park we will look for a place to camp. Then we change to swimming suits and I tell him to have fun. It has never been a problem to let him "be big" and do waterslides on his own. Then about a half hour before the time we have arranged to leave he will come and get me and we will do a couple of waterslides together.

I also let him run at the lumber store or Home Depot. If we get separated he is usually waiting at the car. We do not let him run at a shopping center or a theme park however. In these places he is more interested in keeping track of us than we are worried about losing him.

In an earlier time Steven might have grown up in an institution like "Rain Man" or simply been relegated to the attic. It is normal to be embarrassed in public by his behavior at times, and I would not fault people who would be reluctant to be seen with children like Steven. But long ago I just decided to "own it" and be proud to be Steven's dad. It has paid off. Now some people know me in our small town as "Steven's Dad" and people frequently ask how Steven is doing, even if he is not with me. It is not uncommon for people to know Steven and not me, and they usually tell me what a great guy he is.

One time when we were in Disney World a stranger, a well dressed man who looked like he was part of corporate America, said to me, "You know, I feel sorry for that kid." I looked at Steven, noticed that he was obviously having a better time than some of the younger children around us, and told the man, "You know, I don't."

*Dad teaching Steven to ski.*

*Family outing to Disneyland.*

*Dad and Steven at the waterslide*

*Steve and Dad at Disney World.*

# IN MARK'S OWN WORDS

I am Steven's older brother, Mark, and this is about my experience growing up with Steven. I am about a year and a half older than Steven, so my earliest memories are from when I was still quite young.

What sticks out in my mind most is the memory of going to hospitals when Steven was sick. I have distant, but still vivid, memories of being in a room with my parents while the doctors were looking over x-rays and charts, discussing the diagnosis and options; and my parents were really upset by it all. Since these were dedicated children's hospitals, I also saw all the other sick children we passed in the halls; children in wheelchairs, children with various forms of developmental disabilities, and emaciated children with no hair. It was a very depressing place even then. The staff would sometimes give me toys but I still really hated that place. I did not want to be there.

The other memory I have of my early childhood related to Steven is my time with my maternal grandmother. This was a much better memory, my grandmother being a sweet and generous woman. She also made awesome macaroni and cheese. She helped us when things became too much for my mother. My mother and I spent time with her before Steven was born, when my dad was in Viet Nam in the military. She also took care of Steven and me at her house before anyone knew how ill Steven was. That was when my parents took a trip to Europe. Then, when my mother had to deal with a really sick child, my grandmother helped her out by coming to our house and taking care of me for awhile. Because of this I still have many very good childhood memories of being with her, and of being in Colorado. I think I had my two-year old birthday there, at least I remember blowing out the candles on the cake. I have memories of "playing" croquet in my grandmother's back yard with my uncle, who was in college at the time. I have memories of going on picnics in the mountains, and of smelling the fresh air after an afternoon thunderstorm, which in the summer is almost a daily occurrence in the Rocky Mountains.

That is what I remember of the part of my early childhood that was associated with the problems Steven was having. Eventually he was no longer acutely ill but he was developmentally disabled, probably due to complications from his earlier problems; or perhaps his earlier problems were just the other part of his disability. I don't really know.

In any case, as young children we lived in San Diego, and Steven started attending a private Special Ed school called Los Niños, which means "The Children" in Spanish. Since it was in southern California, I guess it is only natural that it would have a Spanish name. There were, of course, many other children there with similar disabilities, and I remember going there and seeing the children throwing tantrums, banging their heads against the wall, and other things like that.

Steven also had these horrible tantrums at home; he did things like biting and holding one hand in his mouth while flailing the other arm wildly when he was frustrated. Since he lacked fluent language skills it must have been very frustrating to him when he was unable to communicate his wants and needs; much like when a baby cries because he cannot say in words what he wants. This behavior persisted well into adolescence and adulthood. However, as he got older he did gradually mellow out somewhat. Now, in his forties and on some anti-anxiety medication, he has become much more mellow.

When he was younger he also did destructive things to his room, so it wasn't the nicest room to be in because everything was a mess. I think these were also tough times for my parents. He eventually learned to talk, but he has broken autistic speech, and he has his own way of communicating that you have to get used to.

This is also the time when Steven started getting into mischief. All children do to some extent, I think it is part of growing up, to test their boundaries and so on. However, in Steven's case it took a dangerous turn. He would run off if he wasn't constantly supervised, doing things like finding every swimming pool in the neighborhood.

The scariest one I remember is when he nearly fell off the cliff in front of our house. We lived on the oceanfront in Solana Beach, a town about twenty to thirty miles north of San Diego. I lived in this house from the time I was about four or five years old until I was seven and a half years old or so. Steven would have been a year and a half younger. The houses were all overlooking the ocean, perched on an 80 foot high cliff. In front of our house was a deck, beyond that was an ordinary fence and some scrub bushes, and then the drop off from the cliff. One day my mother was panicked because Steven had disappeared again. The next memory I have of this incident was some men pulling Steven up from below the edge of this cliff, all covered in dirt and disheveled. Miraculously, he did not plummet all the way down to the beach.

Another incident occurred when he was a little older, and it was sort of funny if it wasn't so hazardous also. We were at the San Diego Zoo, like we were on many weekends when we lived in San Diego. I was with my dad and Steven; I don't know where my mother was, she was with us on that trip, but I think she had to go to the restroom or something. Somehow Steven ran off and climbed into one of the animal cages, the South American Tapir cage. Fortunately, he did not pick the lion or the tiger cages to go into, but I don't think the Tapir cage was exactly safe either. Tapirs are basically wild pigs with horns, and I can imagine them getting quite aggressive and goring someone if they felt threatened. Anyway, it caused quite a stir. I don't remember how they got Steven out, but he somehow escaped uninjured again. I remember my mom getting angry at my dad when I told her what happened. Sometimes when little kids get excited they just can't keep quiet. So that was a pretty exciting day at the zoo for me, to say the least.

There are a few other times I remember Steven running through the neighborhood. For awhile we had a cabin in Mammoth Lakes, California. This is a ski area that is about a days' drive from southern California. One time when we were there he ran off and I remember the sheriff bringing him back in handcuffs. He wasn't in serious trouble, he just went off to try the elevators at a nearby hotel. That, of course, got people's attention and they called the authorities. The sheriff's deputies didn't know what to do so they handcuffed him, and by that time my parents had made them aware of a missing autistic kid who loved elevators.

It was just before this incident that we had moved to Washington State. I was about eight years old going on nine when we moved. In spite of all these wild stories, by this time I was used to having an autistic brother. Actually, I was used to it from the time I was very young. Except for those early traumatic memories, life growing up with Steven was "my normal". As far as things related to Steven, my adolescence was fairly uneventful. I do not remember any traumatic events that stick out in my mind that happened to Steven. As I said, growing up with a developmentally disabled brother was "my normal". He went to Special Ed at the local high school, and lots of people knew him around town.

One thing about growing up with a severely autistic brother is it comes difficult to get embarrassed in public about pretty much anything. Either people recognized right away that he was autistic or they looked at us oddly. This happened well into adulthood when I was with him, but I learned not to be really concerned or embarrassed about what other people think. If others are unaccepting of him for who he is, then it is their problem, not mine.

Steven also let me and my Dad especially, be a kid for longer than would otherwise be socially acceptable. He loves going to waterparks and Disney World. Before I was married and had a family of my own, I would fly to Seattle, pick him up and we would fly across the country to Orlando, where we would meet my parents and go to Disney World.

*Mark high school graduation.*

*First car.*

# IN GEOFFREY'S OWN WORDS

Growing up as the younger brother of an autistic sibling, my experience was in some ways quite different than that of my parents or my older brother, Mark. While it was a challenge for me just as much as for the rest of my family, I simply never knew anything different and for that reason, abnormal WAS normal. While it had been traumatic for my mother, as well as for my father and older brother, to me it was simply a part of my childhood.

By the time I was born my parents already made one major decision based on our situation that was to additionally shape who I am. They decided to move to a then remote part of Washington state. This constituted an indirect impact on me and my upbringing far greater than the visible drama which comes with an autistic family member.

As much as it seemed that my family was dysfunctional, we actually were a very strong unit when I look back at my childhood. As mentioned earlier, instances such as the public tantrums and obsessive-like behavior by my brother, Steven, while unpleasant, really were not altogether traumatic for me. What I didn't notice as a kid, that now seems to be more consequential to me, was how it altered the actions and behaviors of my other family members.

My Mom and Dad probably were always fairly ambitious people. However, when I look back at my upbringing, I now see how having an autistic child in our household may have led my parents to seek more affluence and social standing than might otherwise have been the case. It possibly led to attempts at overcompensation, and it led them to be workaholics for many years. I suppose that some of that might have been that my Mom and Dad wanted to think about other matters. I probably will never appreciate just how hard it's been on my Mom to raise an autistic child.

My parents had a lot of arguments and disagreements when I was a kid. While it actually may have strengthened their marriage over time, things were usually stressful for everyone in my family in those days. I also still feel guilt at what a pain I could be, not fully realizing just how hard things were for my parents.

They have always tried to give me everything they could and sometimes to a fault. My mother has, at times, gotten almost obsessed about making my life the way she thought was best. As an example, she drove me to the Bainbridge Island ferry dock every morning so I could attend a private school in Seattle. One time she called the school to make sure that I had eaten breakfast! I laugh remembering some of those things, but being overprotective is real, and I simply did not appreciate how worried my Mom was to make sure my life would turn out right. Having had the trauma of giving birth to an autistic son made parenting VERY stressful for her and I just did not fully understand that until well after college.

My Father was often the parent who spent time with Steven, and he made the best of it. I was not deprived of trips to Disneyland as a kid. My Father, Steven and I drove to California numerous times when I was growing up. There are many fathers who I think might have left their families in this situation, or at least would have tried to distance themselves from it. My Dad, with a free day at hand, would take me and Steven to the mall, to the zoo, into Seattle, and other fun places.

I did not fully appreciate the will it took for my Dad to be involved as much as he was, and we often had a difficult relationship when I was a child. When I was age fifteen and in high school, Steven moved into a group home (even though he's always been around during weekends or some of his days off from work). As trite as this may seem, my relationship with my father improved dramatically thereafter. I'm not exactly sure if it was because I'd grown  little older, if it was because my adolescence saw a rift between me and my mother, or if in fact, some degree of stress had just eased from my family.

What I do know is that my parents stepped up to no minor calling in rearing a severely autistic son, and it will be no small challenge for me and my older brother, Mark, to fill their shoes as they grow older.

*Geoff in elementary and high school.*

*Steven, Geoff and Mark at graduation.*

# SOME AFTER-THOUGHTS FROM MOM

From the inception of this project I planned to ask each of my family members to write a short section for my book, sharing their feelings and observations of what it was like to grow up in our family with an autistic brother; and in Phil's case, what it was like to be the father of an autistic child. Each of them readily agreed, saying they would be happy to do that for me. Their instructions were to write anything they wanted about life with Steven and being in our family. They could make it as long or as short as they wanted, but none of them could read what I wrote or what any of the others wrote prior to completing their own "assignment".

It took me approximately five years from start to finish to write this book because I was writing it in "fits and starts", sometimes taking very long breaks in between my writing sessions. I found it difficult to re-live many of the painful memories, and sometimes just needed to wait awhile and think about things before continuing. The longest break happened when Steven became very ill again, and we thought we might lose him. I felt very disheartened for a long time, and almost gave up the project at that time, but Phil urged me not to stop, saying that he thought I would have valuable insights that might be helpful to others.

When I was finally nearing the end of the story, I reminded the family that soon I would need their contributions. Each of them said they remembered, and that they would get their story to me soon. Predictably, Phil finished his first and his was the longest and most comprehensive addition to my story. It also most accurately reflects my recollections of events and my feelings and perceptions of our lives during this time.

Many days, then weeks, and finally several months went by with no progress from Mark and Geoff. They each apologized for taking so long, and offered me their excuses which were valid in part; but I was doing a lot of coaxing, and even asked them if a little monetary compensation might hasten the process. Both immediately refused the offer, stating that it was something they wanted to do for me, and they were a little offended that I would even offer to pay them for it.

Finally, I came to the realization that their problem in part was the same as mine had been; it was difficult for them to dredge up so many of the painful memories again, and in order to write about it, they would need to think about it again and remember how it made them feel at the time.

When I told them I had a deadline since I was finished with the book, they each gave me their story, telling me they really wanted to write more, but decided to give me what they had even though it wasn't as complete as they would have liked.

There are several things that surprised me that both of them said about growing up in our family: They each said that having Steven in our family was their "normal", and that they did not feel deprived of normal family experiences, or that having Steven in the family had made them feel displaced or even "different".

Unsurprisingly, they both knew that Steven's behavior in public could be embarrassing: but both seemingly learned to overcome the embarrassment and not allow it to influence their activities and relationships with others. However, I remember the impact that the movie "Rain Man" had on Mark when he saw it in college. The story was about two brothers, one of whom was autistic, going on a trip to Las Vegas together. The autistic brother was a savant with remembering numbers and the normal brother wanted to use his savant skills to help win money gambling in Las Vegas. There were many humorous and touching scenes along the way, and the movie did an excellent portrayal of an autistic adult's behavior. When this movie became so popular, suddenly there seemed to be a lot of public conversation and acceptance of autism. Having an autistic member in the family was no longer something to be ashamed of, and Mark suddenly seemed less shy when he told his friends about his brother, Steven.

I was surprised to learn that Steven's physical illness involving all of the hospitalizations and surgeries had been so traumatic for Mark. In hindsight, I can see that I was so focused on Steven's life-and-death situations that I was not thinking about Mark and how all of this would affect him. Thankfully, my Mom, his Grandma, stepped in for me and provided the comfort and attention that he needed.

I also was surprised to learn that Geoff felt that he needed to "make up" for Steven's deficiencies by having a perfect life. Since he was the youngest, and since Steven's needs were not as overwhelming as they had been when Mark was little, it is probably true that I was very protective of Geoff, and I also wanted to make sure that I did a better job of meeting his needs than I had been able to do for Mark.

Several of Geoffrey's perceptions, in reality, were not quite what they seemed to him. Phil and I have always been high achievers and our careers had nothing to do with needing to make up for Steven. By the time Geoff was in school, I needed more to do and the family needed more income in order to put both Mark and Geoff through college. I decided to find a career where I could have flexible hours and be home when the children came home from school. I tried selling real estate for awhile but ended up becoming a real estate appraiser and owning my own appraisal business. The business was successful and I was quite busy at times. At the same time, Phil developed a software program and had a small company of his own to market it. In addition, we co-owned some small commercial real estate properties, so between us, we had to juggle our family time.

It is not surprising that the extra stress in our family resulted in more arguments than I believe we would have had otherwise, and that this was also stressful for the children; although Geoffrey mentioned it and Mark did not. This is one of the things that I wish we could go back and change.

It was also interesting that Phil, Mark and I all have vivid memories of the same scary incidents that took place when Steven was younger, most of which happened before Geoffrey was born. Each of us had a slightly different "take11 on things, but all of us were equally impressed with the gravity of the situations.

Many years ago I had asked Liz, the Director of Los Ninos if she was aware of any research regarding how the siblings of autistic children fared later in life. She became very quiet, then told me that yes, some research had been done and that it did indicate that the siblings were impacted by being raised in families with an autistic child, but exact consequences were not really known. My own observations have been that Mark and Geoffrey each exhibited a lack of self-confidence that may have been present in any case, but which I am inclined to attribute to being raised in our family with an autistic brother and with some of the resulting chaos brought about by that fact.

There may also have been some other consequences that have had a subconscious impact on their lives. Mark waited a long time to get married, and when he and his beautiful wife decided that they wanted a child, Mark was worried about whether or not the baby would also be autistic. They did take that leap of faith and they now have a precious normal child and we have an adorable grandson who is loved by all of us. Geoffrey has not decided to get married yet and has also stated that he doesn't want to have children. That may have been his preference in any case, but I feel that it is quite likely related to a fear that he could also have an autistic child.

However, in spite of any negative consequences, my observation is that both Mark and Geoffrey have always been kind, loving and generous to Steven. They have been willing to help with him when asked; and they rarely, if ever, exhibited any jealousy or sibling rivalry. They also are both very accepting and empathetic to others who are different and/or have special needs.

Finally, I had expected all of them, Phil and the two boys, to write more about their feelings; how it felt to be Steven's brother or Steven's dad; and also some of their feelings about what it is like for them now. But I should have known that talking about feelings is not a "guy thing", and it is not surprising that their stories are more a sharing of facts and incidents than of how they felt about all of it.

# PART V

## SOME CLOSING THOUGHTS

# AUTISM: THEN AND NOW

The word "autism" originally comes from the Greek word "autos" which means "self", and in about 1908 "autism" was used by a Swiss psychiatrist to describe the symptoms of a subset of a population of persons diagnosed as schizophrenic.

In 1943 an American psychiatrist, Dr. Leo Kanner, used the term to describe the symptoms of a small group of children that he was treating, and he described the children with these symptoms as having "early infantile autism", because they developed the symptoms in the first 30 months of life. For a time, this disorder was known as "Kanner's Syndrome". Shortly after this, a German scientist named Hans Asperger delineated a milder form of autism, which is now known as Asperger's Syndrome.

In 1967 Dr. Bruno Bettelheim published a book based on his observations of patients at an institution which treated children with emotional disorders; putting forth the theory that autism was caused by "refrigerator mothers". It was thought that these mothers had totally rejected their own child; that the mothers were cold and unfeeling, and that they were unable to give love and affection to the child. You can imagine how unbearable this must have been for the parents of an autistic child, especially the mother. Not only did she have to deal with an extremely difficult child, but she also had to endure excruciating guilt as result of society's attitude and belief that she had caused the problem.

Today the label used to describe the disorder is ASD, or Autism Spectrum Disorder. This is probably the most accurate term found so far to describe it. Those diagnosed as having the disorder present a wide range of symptoms, and demonstrate levels of functioning from very severely impaired to those who are able to function at a nearly normal level.

When Steven was diagnosed, many people including our relatives and friends, had very little understanding or knowledge about what it meant to be autistic. After a while I was able to come up with some creative ways to describe it to them. I told them that it was like a continuum, and those who were very severely affected were at the low end of the continuum, while the very high functioning individuals were at the top of the continuum. Steven was diagnosed as classically autistic, and his level of functioning as a child was at the lower end of the continuum. As an adult his level of functioning falls someplace in the lower-middle of the continuum. Today we would substitute the word "spectrum" for "continuum" and have the same understanding of the meaning.

I also gleaned from my reading that it was useful to describe these children as being "functionally deaf and blind". Although they are able to hear sounds and see things around them, their brains are unable to make the connections for these incoming sensory stimuli in the same way that a normal person does. I used the story of Helen Keller as an example; noting that Steven's behavior was very similar to Helen Keller's before Helen found the wonderful teacher who saved her life. Helen's world was similar to that of an autistic child; frightening and unfamiliar, and without help she was unable to make sense of anything going on around her. Her response was to throw screaming temper tantrums, the same as non-verbal autistic children do. Once a method was found to teach Helen how to "see" and "hear" in her world, she was then able to learn how to communicate with others and to lead a meaningful life in spite of her severe disabilities. Once more, this is analogous to the changes in the behavior of autistic children when they start to learn language and are able to better communicate with others.

The other example I used to describe what Steven's world was like for him, was asking one to imagine being in a foreign country where the language and customs were completely different from anything you had ever experienced, and to imagine how scary and frustrating that might be. Everything in that world would be unpredictable, and no one would be able to explain to you what was going on around you. You would feel alone and overwhelmed, much as Steven's world seemed to him.

It was much more likely 40 years ago that an autistic child would be institutionalized for life. We were on the cutting edge of research that was developing treatment strategies that allowed these children to progress to the point that many, if not most, were able to function in normal society without the need for an institution. Attitudes were also changing about most disabilities, and the prevailing thought was starting to change toward more acceptance of keeping these children in normal home settings and providing what was known as "the least restrictive environment" for them.

There has always been a great deal of discussion about the causes of autism, and as yet, there are no definitive answers. Many studies have been done regarding inherited genetic causes but so far it is not possible to do genetic testing prior to birth to detect this disorder or to predict it prior to pregnancy. There have also been numerous theories about other causes, such as diseases during pregnancy or early childhood, or toxic environmental factors.

One of the possible causes that has generated a great deal of controversy is the rubella measles vaccine. Thankfully, the medical profession has incontrovertibly debunked this theory. It was found that the research was skewed and defective, and there are few, if any physicians who would give any credence at all to this theory of causation. This belief has given rise to an increase in the actual incidence of Rubella because many parents still believe it and have refused to have their children vaccinated.

There is greater reason to believe that the actual Rubella disease might be a cause of autism. There is a condition known as Rubella Syndrome which is caused by the Rubella infection. If an unborn child is exposed to Rubella through the mother being infected, especially in the early months of pregnancy, the infant has a high likelihood of being born blind, deaf, severely retarded and having serious heart defects. Therefore, when parents do not vaccinate their children for this preventable disease, they are increasing the incidence of Rubella Syndrome in the general population, and therefore contributing to the possible increase in autism.

There are other theories that today there is more exposure to toxic substances in the environment and that this is leading to a higher prevalence of autism, but to date no known substances in the environment have been proven to cause autism.

Probably there are multiple causations of the disorder, and any of those discussed here could be causative factors. Whatever the cause, the number of cases of diagnosed autism has increased greatly over Steven's lifetime. When Steven was diagnosed, the belief was that four in 10,000 children suffered from this disorder, and that boys were 10 times more likely to have it than girls. Today the incidence of autism has proved to be far greater; figures from the CDC estimate it to be as many as 1 in 68 persons in the United States diagnosed as having some form of autism.

My personal belief is that one of the primary reasons for the significant increase in the incidence of autism is that today there is a greater awareness of the disorder, particularly in the professional and medical communities that serve the needs of this population. In the past many children went undiagnosed. Parents and professionals alike were puzzled by the array of symptoms that autistic children display, and these children often went undiagnosed or misdiagnosed for many years.

An example is a young man that I first met when we moved to Washington State. He was assigned to a Special Ed class, so I met his mother, Gael. After she observed Steven for a short time, she asked me if I thought her son also might be autistic. She told me that doctors and other professionals over the years had been unable to identify his disorder. I observed him for a very short period of time, and almost immediately I recognized the telltale signs that would indicate a very high functioning autistic person. He was eleven years old at the time, so there had been many years during which no one had been able to give Gael an accurate diagnosis, and which in turn had resulted in inadequate treatment and educational services for him.

The ability to more accurately diagnose people with autism and the increased awareness of the disorder has also led to an increase in available funding for research and treatment. These are positive developments and provide more hope for the future of those affected by autism.

At the time when Steven was diagnosed there were also very few resources available for parents who were struggling with the problems of raising a child with autism. In addition to Steven's pioneering treatment center, Los Niños, the only other major resource available was the National Society for Autistic Children. It was founded in 1965 by a parent of an autistic child, Bernard Rimland, PhD. This was the earliest organization with a membership primarily of parents but it also included some professionals who were involved in early research efforts and treatment strategies. It was a support group for parents, and my attendance at one of their early conferences strongly influenced the beginning of my recovery, giving me hope for our future with Steven.

Today there are two major organizations providing resources for parents and others involved with autism. When NSAC was formed, many of the parents who were members at the time had very young children, and as these children became adults it was apparent that the needs of the autistic population did not end with childhood. Adulthood brought the need for new services and different ways to address the problems, and thus the name of the organization was changed in 1987 to "Autism Society of America".

In 2005 another organization was founded called "Autism Speaks" by a grandmother of an autistic child, Suzanne Wright. This organization has an international presence and also provides help to parents in the form of information and resources.

Both of these organizations serve an important function for people with autism of every age. They are both involved in advocacy for services, they both help to fund research, and they both provide referral services for anyone needing help in meeting the needs of someone with autism. They each have a web site for those who are interested in their services.

It is reassuring to me as a parent, who has struggled with obtaining appropriate services for many years, to see the quality and quantity of help available today.

# THE FUTURE

None of us knows what the future holds; not for Steven nor for the possibility of finding a cure for this distressing disorder. The greatest fear for every parent of a special needs child is, "What will happen to my child when I am gone?" As Phil and I learned over time, and much to our surprise, the child may be sharing this fear. As Steven got older, especially after he began to understand the meaning of death, he began talking to us about it, saying, "When Mom and Dad get too old and die?", his way of asking how long would it be before this happened. At the same time he started to recognize that Mom and Dad were not invincible, and started to worry about our well being.

For example, on one of our vacations with Steven about two years ago, we spent the last day in Orlando at Sea World, one of his favorite places. It was during the Christmas holiday season and the park was extremely crowded. We were walking along the sidewalk when a small child suddenly darted in front of me; I tripped and fell face down on the hard surface. I hit my head in the fall and was not immediately okay. I had minor injuries and some bleeding from cuts that required ice and bandages; and I needed to sit quietly for about 30 minutes to regain my equilibrium. However, I was fine after the cuts and bruises healed.

Ever since this event, whenever we are with Steven walking in a crowded place, he always grabs my hand, stating, "Mom no go boom, Mom be okay". He is very concerned about letting us out of his sight in public places saying, "Steven no lose Dad." He also carefully tracks our whereabouts when we are not with him, checking our calendar when he is home, and memorizing the dates that we will be away. He then calls us on his cell phone, and wants to know where we are and what we are doing.

When we realized how concerned he was about the future, we tried to be reassuring, telling him that it would be many years before Mom and Dad were "too old", and that Mark would be there to help him when we were gone. So now he talks about going to

California to live near Mark when we are gone, and he seems satisfied that he will be okay when this happens. Fortunately, both of his brothers have volunteered without hesitation to look after Steven and make sure that he is taken care of when we are no longer able. We know that they love him and will gladly do this, but we are also concerned that they are able to lead normal lives of their own and are not overly burdened with caring for Steven.

The discussion of autism would not be complete without talking about research. As parents of an autistic child, we always hold out the hope that there might be a breakthrough in research and treatment of the disorder during the lifetime of our child; but we also realize that we must accept the reality of living with the disorder today, and we must continue to utilize the very best treatment methods that are currently available. In this regard, we have had many requests for Steven to participate in various research programs. As long as there were no physically intrusive or painful tests involved, we have always been willing to cooperate. We know that probably none of these projects will directly benefit Steven, but we are hopeful that some of these tests might contribute to finding a cure at some future date that will significantly improve the lives of others affected by this disorder.

My message to the parents of autistic children who are either just embarking on this journey, or who are still trying to struggle through it, is to never give up the hope that there will be a cure found in the lifetime of your child. Medical research is expanding exponentially and there is a good possibility that a cure will be found, maybe sooner rather than later.

At the same time, take advantage of all of the services and any of the treatment strategies that show promise for helping you deal with the present realities, so that both you and your autistic child can lead as normal a life as possible. Know also that in your darkest days there is a light at the end of the tunnel. These children do not stay the same forever. They grow up and there are many changes for the better as they get older, particularly now that we have learned how to change their behaviors, and with the changing attitudes in society about this disorder. Don't ever be afraid to reach out to others for support when you need it, because there are many wonderful and understanding people out there who are ready and willing to help.

Most of all, love and enjoy your child. Even though these children have greater challenges growing up, it is such a joy to watch them succeed along the way.

*Steven as a baby and in elementary school.*

*Steven in high school.*

*Mark, Geoff and Steven.*

# LETTERS TO MY CHILDREN

Dear Mark and Geoffrey,

The primary reason that I wrote this story was so that you would understand some of the things that happened in our family from a Mom's perspective and so that you would know how very much we loved each and every one of you children.

Each of you is a precious gift from God, and we wanted to do the very best that we could to make sure that you would grow up to be happy adults who understand and appreciate the deeper meanings of life. We wanted you to learn to find happiness through giving to others and making a positive contribution to society. We wanted you to be able to follow your dreams and to be able to have loving and positive relationships with others in your lives. We tried to give you as many tools as we could so that when it was time for you to make your own way, you would be well prepared.

However, we were not perfect parents and we made many mistakes along the way. There are things I wish we could go back and undo, things that we should have done differently. I know and understand how difficult it was for you to grow up in our family. It was difficult for us as the adults and parents to understand and deal with many of the problems, so we can imagine how hard it was for you as small children. There were times, especially when Steven was younger, that were extremely chaotic, and these times were distressing for all of us, but especially for you. We hope that as adults now yourselves that you can understand some of these times and forgive us for the mistakes that we made.

There were many times when I know that Steven received the lion's share of my time, and I felt very guilty about not spending more time with you, but even today I don't know how that could have been remedied. Your Grandma, my Mom, also loved all of us and she was a wonderful substitute for me during times that I was absolutely unable to spend the time needed to take care of you. All of us will always remember and be grateful for her love.

I also know that you both love your brother, Steven, very much, and I want to tell you thank-you for the times you spent patiently helping us take care of him. I do not remember either of you being anything other than patient and understanding with Steven. You always treated him with kindness and generosity; I really don't remember any meanness or anger towards him.

So my hope and wish is that the main take-away of your childhood years is that in spite of the difficult times you feel like we do, that knowing Steven and having him in our family has greatly enriched our lives. He has taught all of us to appreciate the differences in all people, to be thankful for the blessings we have and to appreciate and understand those who are different and have extra challenges in life.

Love, Mom

-----

Dear Steven,

I know that what I have written about the story of your life growing up in our family is something that you can't understand and appreciate right now and maybe never, unless a cure is found for autism in your lifetime. But my message to you is the same as it is to Mark and Geoffrey, we love you so very much and only want you to be happy. Your happiness is found in different ways than theirs, but our goal for you is the same, that you find fulfillment in your life in whatever you are able to do.

You have brought joy and happiness into our lives, and you have enriched us in so many ways. We have learned to have more tolerance and patience than we would ever have imagined possible. We have learned to appreciate those who are different from us and those who are more challenged in being able to navigate their way through life. We also have learned to appreciate the people in our lives who have shown such love and dedication to you.

Most of all we want you to know how much you are loved and cherished by all of us; your two brothers, your Mom and your Dad.

Love, Mom

And finally a note to my husband, Phil:

The children were my inspiration for this story but you were my encouragement. When I first mentioned the idea of writing it, you told me it was a great idea, and when I faltered along the way, taking a break and not being sure that I wanted to continue, you encouraged me to finish.

We embarked on this journey together, and when the going got rough, it sometimes looked as though we would break. But our love for our children and each other carried us through. We both know that there will continue to be the ups and the downs; I never promised you a rose garden, nor you me, but together we will continue to love our children and now our extended family that includes a beautiful daughter-in-law and an adorable grandchild, with all of our hearts until the end of this journey of life.

# ACKNOWLEDGMENTS

The highest level of gratitude is owed to my good friend and my editor, Louisa Beckett. She generously volunteered her time to do the tedious work of checking grammar, spelling and punctuation, as well as giving me thoughtful suggestions for improving readability without changing the story.

I also want to give posthumous recognition to two special mothers. Louisa's mother, Anne Rudeen, was the first to read the beginning half of my manuscript and she strongly encouraged me to continue writing the book. Anne, who was a published author herself, was the one who suggested that the inclusion of many pictures would greatly enhance the story. Sadly she passed away this past summer without ever having had the opportunity to read the finished book, but I believe that she would have been pleased at the result.

The other mother to whom I owe the greatest gratitude is my own, Anita Wagner, who in addition to giving us her unconditional love, took most of the pictures that have been included in the book. She was an amateur photographer who spent many hours perfecting her skills, and without her photos our family album would have been scant indeed, as neither Phil nor I had the time to take pictures when our children were growing up. We were both overwhelmed just taking care of everyone's daily needs. Like Anne, my mother is no longer alive, but I think she would have been pleased to see her photos included in my book about our family.

Appreciation is also owed to my family; my husband, Phil, and my sons, Mark and Geoffrey. They not only contributed directly to the book with their own stories about Steven, but they also were willing to share our private story with the outside world. We all realized that in so doing we were opening the door to possible misunderstanding and criticism, but when considering the potential for helping others, we all felt that the positives far outweighed the possible negatives.

Last, but certainly not least, I wish to thank my publisher, Ingemar Anderson and his entire team at Kitsap Publishing for tending to the many details that transformed my raw manuscript into the finished product, this book.